MW00633245

Caring School Community™

# Schoolwide Community-Building Activities

DEVELOPMENTAL STUDIES CENTER™

Developmental Studies Center
2000 Embarcadero, Suite 305
Oakland, CA 94606-5300
(800) 666-7270, fax: (510) 464-3670
www.devstu.org

ISBN-13: 978-1-57621-523-4
ISBN-10: 1-57621-523-7

Printed in the United States of America

2 3 4 5 6 7 8 9 10

Funding for Developmental Studies Center has been generously provided by:

The Annenberg Foundation, Inc.

The Atlantic Philanthropies (USA) Inc.

The Robert Bowne Foundation, Inc.

The Annie E. Casey Foundation

Center for Substance Abuse Prevention:
Substance Abuse and Mental Health Services Agency,
U.S. Department of Health and Human Services

The Danforth Foundation

The DuBarry Foundation

The Ford Foundation

William T. Grant Foundation

Evelyn and Walter Haas, Jr. Fund

Walter and Elise Haas Fund

J. David and Pamela Hakman Family Foundation

Hasbro Children's Foundation

Charles Hayden Foundation

The William Randolph Hearst Foundation

Clarence E. Heller Charitable Foundation

The William and Flora Hewlett Foundation

The James Irvine Foundation

The Robert Wood Johnson Foundation

Walter S. Johnson Foundation

Ewing Marion Kauffman Foundation

W.K. Kellogg Foundation

John S. and James L. Knight Foundation

Lilly Endowment, Inc.

The MBK Foundation

Mr. and Mrs. Sanford N. McDonnell

The John D. and Catherine T. MacArthur Foundation

A.L. Mailman Family Foundation, Inc.

Charles Stewart Mott Foundation

National Institute on Drug Abuse (NIDA),
National Institutes of Health

National Science Foundation

Nippon Life Insurance Foundation

Karen and Christopher Payne Foundation

The Pew Charitable Trusts

The Pinkerton Foundation

The Rockefeller Foundation

Louise and Claude Rosenberg, Jr. Family Foundation

The San Francisco Foundation

Shinnyo-En Foundation

Silver Giving Foundation

The Spencer Foundation

Spunk Fund, Inc.

Stuart Foundation

The Stupski Family Foundation

The Sulzberger Foundation, Inc.

Surdna Foundation, Inc.

John Templeton Foundation

U.S. Department of Education

Wallace-Reader's Digest Funds

Wells Fargo Bank

# Table of Contents


## Preface

PART 1 **Refocusing Schoolwide Activities** ........ 1

PART 2 **Getting Started: Leadership** ........ 7

PART 3 **Activities That Build Community** ........ 15

**Getting To Know the People in Our School** ........ 16

*Activity 1: People Who Make It Work* ........ 17

*Activity 2: Welcoming Newcomers* ........ 21

*Activity 3: Buddies Program* ........ 24

**Getting To Know the People in Our Community** ........ 28

*Activity 4: Family Heritage Museum* ........ 29

*Activity 5: Family Projects Fair* ........ 34

*Activity 6: Grandpersons Gathering* ........ 41

**Expanding Our Community** ........ 46

*Activity 7: Adopt-a-Family* ........ 47

*Activity 8: Working for a Cause* ........ 52

**Sharing What We Learn** ........ 54

*Activity 9: Family Read-Aloud* ........ 55

*Activity 10: Family Science Night* ........ 59

*Activity 11: Family Math* ........ 62

*Activity 12: Family Film Night* ........ 66

**Taking Pride in Our Surroundings** ........ 70

*Activity 13: Litter Critters* ........ 71

*Activity 14: Schoolwide Mural* ........ 73

*Activity 15: School Community Garden* ........ 77

PART 4 **Suggestions for Teachers** ........ 83

*Activity 1: People Who Make It Work* ........ 85

*Activity 2: Welcoming Newcomers* ........ 87

*Activity 3: Buddies Program* ........ 89

*Activity 4: Family Heritage Museum* ........ 92

*Activity 5: Family Projects Fair* ........ 94

*Activity 6: Grandpersons Gathering* ........ 96

*Activity 7: Adopt-a-Family* ........ 100

*Activity 8: Working for a Cause* ........ 102

*Activity 10: Family Science Night* ........ 104

*Activity 13: Litter Critters* ........ 106

*Activity 14: Schoolwide Mural* ........ 108

*Activity 15: School Community Garden* ........ 110

PART 5 **Resources** ........ 113

*Schoolwide Community-Building: A Needs Assessment*

*Schoolwide Activity Assessment*

*Questions for the Coordinating Team : How Are We Doing?*

*Strategies for Increasing Parent Involvement*

*Additional Schoolwide Activities*

# Preface

This book is about something all schools are concerned with — creating community. It reflects the work of thousands of teachers, administrators, children, and parents who have collaborated with Developmental Studies Center (DSC) over the past decades to create the Caring School Community™ (CSC) program. CSC is designed to help elementary schools become inclusive, caring communities and stimulating, supportive places to learn. The schoolwide activities described in this book are just one component of CSC.

Our research shows that for children to reach their fullest social and academic potential, they need

- close and caring relationships with their peers and teachers;
- opportunities to practice and benefit from prosocial values;
- challenging, relevant curriculum; and
- close cooperation and communication between families and school staff.

To create such an environment, CSC involves teachers, administrators, and parents in creating "caring communities of learners" in schools and classrooms—communities in which children are encouraged to care about each other and about their learning. The program incorporates constructivist learning theory, cooperative learning techniques, classroom and schoolwide community-building strategies, and an approach to classroom management that helps students develop self-control and a commitment to fundamental values such as fairness, helpfulness, caring, and responsibility.

We would like to thank the people who contributed ideas to this publication, especially Denise Wood, Suzanne Antoine, Michele Brynjulson, and Pam Solomon for their pioneering efforts to make parents integral to their school communities.

The organization and writing of this book has been managed by Amy Schoenblum, with important contributions from Josie Arce and Rosa Zubizarreta. Lynn Murphy and Anne Goddard have provided editorial advice and assistance. Jeff Puda Design provided the graphic design.

Funding to support this and other programs of Developmental Studies Center has been provided by the following:

The Annenberg Foundation, Inc.
The Atlantic Philanthropies (USA) Inc.
The Robert Bowne Foundation, Inc.
The Annie E. Casey Foundation
Center for Substance Abuse Prevention, Substance Abuse and Mental Health Services Agency, U.S. Department of Health and Human Services
The Danforth Foundation
The DuBarry Foundation
The Ford Foundation
Evelyn and Walter Haas, Jr. Fund
Walter and Elise Haas Fund
J. David & Pamela Hakman Family Foundation
Hasbro Children's Foundation
Charles Hayden Foundation
The William Randolph Hearst Foundation
Clarence E. Heller Charitable Foundation
The William and Flora Hewlett Foundation
The James Irvine Foundation
The Robert Wood Johnson Foundation
Walter S. Johnson Foundation
Ewing Marion Kauffman Foundation
W.K. Kellogg Foundation
John S. and James L. Knight Foundation
Lilly Endowment, Inc.
The MBK Foundation
Mr. & Mrs. Sanford N. McDonnell
The John D. and Catherine T. MacArthur Foundation
A.L. Mailman Family Foundation, Inc.
Charles Stewart Mott Foundation
National Institute on Drug Abuse (NIDA), National Institutes of Health
National Science Foundation
Nippon Life Insurance Foundation
The Pew Charitable Trusts
The Pinkerton Foundation
The Rockefeller Foundation
Louise and Claude Rosenberg, Jr. Family Foundation
The San Francisco Foundation
Shinnyo-En Foundation
Silver Giving Foundation
The Spencer Foundation
Spunk Fund, Inc.
Stuart Foundation
The Stupski Family Foundation
The Sulzberger Foundation, Inc.
Surdna Foundation, Inc.
U.S. Department of Education
Wallace–Reader's Digest Funds
Wells Fargo Bank

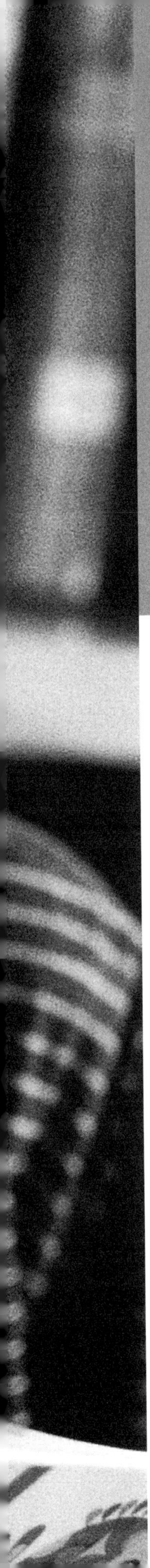

# 1 Refocusing Schoolwide Activities

Schoolwide activities play a major role in reinforcing or undermining a school's goals. For this reason, adults in the school need to make a conscious decision to reinforce what's really important, and to create activities that are inclusive, support children's learning, foster an appreciation of differences, and provide children with the opportunity to help others.

# Creating a Sense of Community

While many of the community-building ideas presented here will be familiar, what may be new is the emphasis on the relationships that form and foster a sense of community—relationships that include everyone, avoid competition, and respect differences but lessen hierarchical divisions between older and younger students, staff members and students, and teachers and parents. As you read the pages that follow, think about your goals for community building and about the schoolwide activities your school already sponsors. Then think about ways in which small shifts in focus may better align these activities with your goals.

## Focus on Relationships

A school community is a set of relationships: among children, among school staff members, among staff members and children, and among staff members and children's families. In a caring community, these relationships are valued, supported, and nurtured. Of course, these relationships can exist independent of a comprehensive effort by the school to support them, but they are more likely to flourish when community-building is a consciously held goal of every member of the school. And whether or not we make community-building an explicit part of a school's curriculum, children interact with others and absorb lessons about how to get along with others every day they are in school—so of course we'd like to be sure they're in an environment where they're absorbing "good" lessons. Our goal is to help schools create an atmosphere of care and trust, so that children can develop as caring, principled individuals. The more children feel that their school community cares about them and meets their needs, the more likely they are to feel attached to that community, to practice the values it promotes, and to thrive academically and socially.

## Prepare for Synergy

Both the beauty and challenge of community-building is how interrelated your efforts can be. You may undertake a community service project to teach children about helping others (disaster victims, for example), and then realize that there are few opportunities for children to help each other at school. Why not create some? You may plan a cooperative family projects fair, and then realize that your honor roll bumper stickers encourage families to compete with each other over their children's grade cards. What message do you want to convey about competition? You may ask children to devise specific ways to welcome new students to the school, but have no plan for helping new staff members feel at home. How can all newcomers be welcomed into the school community?

At times this picture of creating a caring community can seem overwhelming. But it can also be enormously energizing. We encourage you to start small and let thoughtful reflection about your goals point the way.

## Essential Ingredients: Add a Community-Building Twist

Every school has its favorite programs—sports events, picnics, award ceremonies, canned food drives, and so on. While many of these programs are enjoyable and foster a spirit of community, others have the potential to exclude some students and their families, promote unnecessary competition, or create disappointment when children don't succeed or win.

This book invites you to take a look at the events that are traditional within your school and give them a community-building "twist" so that they demonstrate and reinforce the values of a caring community. When we ask schools to tell us how their activities reinforce these values, they describe several "essential ingredients" that shape their efforts. Take a moment to consider these ingredients, or values, as you begin to think about the activities at your school.

### *ESSENTIAL INGREDIENTS*

**1 Inclusion and Participation**

- All parents, children, and school staff members are invited to participate freely in schoolwide activities, particularly those designed for families to enjoy together.
- Invitations are warm, welcoming, and nonthreatening.
- Activities are designed with attention to special language, cultural, economic, and child care needs of participating families.

**2 Cooperative Environment**

- Children and families are able to enjoy cooperative, noncompetitive activities that promote the value of learning together and helping others.
- Everyone succeeds at learning; there are no losers.

**3 Emphasis on Helping Others and Taking Responsibility**

- Children are given the opportunity to experience the value of helping others.
- Everyone takes responsibility within and outside the school community.

**4 Appreciation of Differences**

- Parents, children, and school staff members feel that their social and cultural backgrounds are valued and respected within the school community.
- Everyone is encouraged to share his or her cultural heritage and learn from others.

**5 Reflection**

- Everyone is encouraged to reflect on what has been learned from the experience of working together.

Consider the following example of how these essential ingredients might be realized in an actual activity, such as your school's annual science fair. How can the "traditional" science fair—in which children compete to create the "best" project in the hope of winning an award—be adapted to create an environment where everyone is included, everyone works cooperatively, and everyone wins?

**TRADITIONAL VS. NONCOMPETITIVE**

| **"Traditional" Science Fair** | **Noncompetitive Science Fair** |
|---|---|
| Individual students create science projects that are displayed in a central area, such as a gym or library. Students and families view the projects. Prizes are awarded to "outstanding" projects. | Science experiments and activities are set up around the school in different classrooms. Students and families visit the classrooms and try out the activities. Students and families become more comfortable in school and experience a collaborative learning atmosphere—everyone is a learner. |
| competitive | collaborative |
| goal is to win | goal is to participate |
| students work individually | students work with families and other students |
| parents observe | parents participate |
| teachers judge | teachers participate |
| some people win, some people lose | everyone wins, no one loses |
| excludes students and families unwilling to compete | includes everyone |

## How To Use This Book

We ask you once again to reflect on this simple idea: that a school community is a set of relationships among children, among school staff members, among staff members and children, and among staff members and children's families. This book helps you build a caring community in which these relationships are valued, supported, and nurtured throughout the school.

Part 2 suggests ways to get started and get people involved in your school community-building efforts. You will find the ideas about assessing your school needs and schoolwide activities especially helpful for staying focused on what contributes to building a caring community and what may detract from it. (We've also provided several tools in Part 5 to help your school in the planning process.)

Part 3 describes specific activities that build community, which are organized into five sections:

- *Getting To Know the People in Our School* offers ways for students and staff members to learn more about one another.
- *Getting To Know the People in Our Community* brings family members into the school and deepens what we mean by "getting to know" someone.
- *Expanding Our Community* further widens the circle of community and reminds everyone that communities are generous to others, not only to the people within their immediate group.
- *Sharing What We Learn* allows students and teachers to share their academic and social learning goals with students' families through events such as read-aloud nights and cooperative science fairs.
- *Taking Pride in Our Surroundings* suggests activities that build pride in the school environment and make it a pleasant place for everyone.

Part 4 offers Suggestions for Teachers specific to the schoolwide activities—ideas for introducing activities, executing the classroom component of projects, connecting projects to curriculum areas, helping students reflect on the activity and related ideas, follow-up activities, and so on. These resource pages can easily be photocopied and distributed to staff members, to be discussed at staff meetings and used in the classroom.

Part 5 is a collection of resources that may be useful to you as you begin to plan and coordinate community-building efforts at your school. Feel free to photocopy them as needed.

Many more activities can be added to those recommended here, and we hope you will experiment with your own ideas. We invite you to use this book as a resource and springboard for building your own unique community. Consider the suggestions described here, then take an idea and try it out!

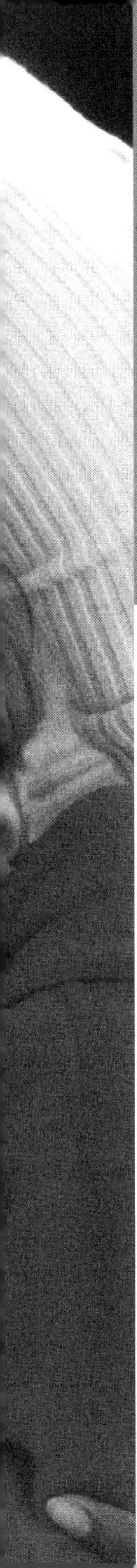

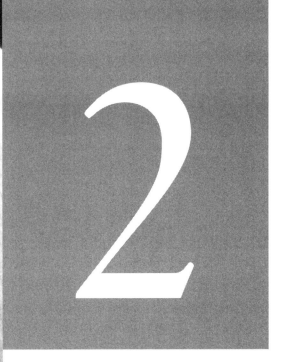

# 2 Getting Started: Leadership

CSC schools with successful community-building programs emphasize the importance of effective leadership for the effort. Most schools have entrusted the conceptualization, planning, and implementation of their schoolwide program to a Coordinating Team—a diverse group of individuals representing all constituencies of the school community.

# Developing a Team Approach

The key to building effective leadership is including and involving representatives from the major groups within the school—parents, teachers, administrators, school staff, and in some instances, upper-grade students. In a caring school community, all members should feel included and valued for their participation.

---

## Role of the Coordinating Team

The Coordinating Team is responsible for leading the way toward building a more caring school community. As the keeper of the school's vision of the kind of community it would like to be, and as the leadership group that makes things happen, the team's main functions are to:

- ***assess the needs*** of the existing school community
- ***create a vision*** of the school as a community and set goals and benchmarks for the year
- ***communicate*** the vision and possible activities to other members of the school community, asking for their suggestions
- ***plan and coordinate*** schoolwide activities
- ***assess each activity*** and overall progress toward goals

## Role of the Principal

In addition to healthy collaborative relationships among its members, the Coordinating Team's success depends upon the full support and commitment of the principal. The principal must be willing to give the team access to financial, human, and material resources and must provide time for members of the team to work together. Perhaps most important, the principal must model the collaborative and risk-taking behaviors she or he wants to encourage in the team—for example, the willingness to work together and try out new things, even if those experiments might not go perfectly at first.

## Communicating Your Purpose and Goals

Creating a dynamic and successful Coordinating Team will be easier if you begin with a look at existing parent and faculty committees, leadership opportunities, and the process for making decisions that affect the entire school. Consider sponsoring discussions with existing committees so that efforts will be less likely to duplicate each other and more likely to capitalize on the potential for collaboration and communication. (This is particularly important if decisions at your school are made by committees or teams.) It is also important that the relationship of the Coordinating Team to each of the relevant committees be well defined, so that goals and responsibilities for the year are agreed upon by all.

We encourage you to hold an open meeting to introduce the idea of focusing schoolwide activities on the values of a caring community and to invite members of the school community to join the Coordinating Team (see sample below). Such a meeting can help parents, teachers, and staff understand what you are trying to accomplish and why, and is likely to build support for the effort.

**SAMPLE** ***LETTER TO FAMILIES***

Dear Family Members and Family Friends,

This year at (NAME) School we are making a special effort to have our school be a place where children feel comfortable, cared for, and included. We want children's family members to feel especially welcome here, too. We are calling our effort **Schoolwide Community-Building** and the idea is to refocus our existing schoolwide activities (and create new ones) so that all of us, adults and children, feel that we are part of a caring school community.

There will be many opportunities to participate in activities with your children and to be involved at school. You will receive information throughout the year, but you can also help us now by joining a Coordinating Team of parents and school staff who will create and organize community-building activities for the year.

We'd like to invite you to an open meeting to learn more about Schoolwide Community-Building, add your ideas, and consider how you might participate. If you're interested in being on the Coordinating Team, or simply helping out, please join us!

(day), (date)
(TIME)–(TIME) p.m.
(NAME) School Cafeteria
Child care will be provided.

## Creating the Coordinating Team

Again, we encourage you to begin by issuing an open invitation to parents, teachers, administrators, and other school staff interested in participating on the Coordinating Team. Although every school's team will look and feel unique, most CSC schools recommend having an equal number of parent and teacher members representing several grade levels and the diversity of ethnic, racial, linguistic, and social groups that comprise the school community. The goal is to create a team that is truly representative of the makeup of the school community.

| 'MODEL' OF A COORDINATING TEAM |
|---|
| 3–4 parents |
| 3–4 teachers |
| 1 nonteaching staff member |
| 1 principal |
| 1 head custodian |
| 1 part-time coordinator (paid or volunteer) |

Schools we have worked with strongly recommend enlisting a parent to act as a part-time coordinator for the team—someone who gets things started, locates resources, manages the budget, makes sure that everyone is informed about upcoming activities, and keeps a record of what occurs. In a few cases, schools have been able to use school improvement funds or grants to hire this coordinator, adding further support and credibility to their community-building efforts. Another option is to have a program resource teacher, counselor, or teacher "released" from a portion of his or her responsibilities to serve this function for a few hours each week.

While you are in the first stages of creating a Coordinating Team, consider some general questions about the structure and function of the team—questions about recruiting team members, building an effective team, staying focused, communicating with each other and the school community, and reflecting on the team activities. Questions for the Coordinating Team, which can be found in Part 5, the Resources section of this book, suggests the important questions that might be asked about and by the Coordinating Team; you will probably want to revisit these questions with the whole team from time to time.

## Planning a Schoolwide Program

Many CSC schools recommend beginning the year with a one-day retreat for the Coordinating Team, so that team members can get to know each other, develop a set of goals and priorities for the year, decide which activities will help reach these goals, and create a timeline and action plan for the year.

The Coordinating Team retreat is also a good time to create a working budget. We encourage you to find creative ways to apply school improvement funds, special grants, PTA resources, and other funding to your community-building efforts.

In planning an array of activities for the school year, the Coordinating Team balances several concerns: How many activities can we manage? What can the budget support? How many other events—such as school plays, chorus recitals, and grade-card conferences—already involve parents and their schedules? Can any of these be given a CSC twist? Where will we have the biggest impact?

**COORDINATING TEAM PLANNING**

**1 Avoid Turf Confusion**

- Review existing committees, leadership structures, and decision-making processes

**2 Build Support**

- Present ideas at open meeting for teachers, parents, administrators, and other school staff
- Solicit Coordinating Team membership

**3 Gather Information**

- Collect responses to Schoolwide Community-Building: A Needs Assessment Survey

**4 Convene Coordinating Team**

- Select Coordinator
- As a group address Questions for the Coordinating Team

**5 Hold One-Day Planning Retreat**

- Review needs assessment
- Brainstorm possible schoolwide activities
- Evaluate proposed activities with Schoolwide Activity Assessment
- Allocate budget
- Set timeline

Two tools provided in Part 5 can be very helpful to Coordinating Teams as they set goals and priorities: Schoolwide Community-Building: A Needs Assessment is a survey that helps schools identify their current strengths and weaknesses in building community; and a Schoolwide Activity Assessment helps gauge a specific activity's appropriateness and potential for meeting the school's community-building needs.

Before the Coordinating Team retreat, have adults and children from all segments of the school community fill out the Schoolwide Community-Building survey to "take the pulse" of the community and identify patterns that may exist. At the retreat, the results of the survey can be used to generate discussion and shape long- and short-term goals for schoolwide activities and community building.

Having set these goals, the Coordinating Team can use the Schoolwide Activity Assessment to choose and design particular activities. The assessment asks questions that highlight the necessary considerations for effective and suitable schoolwide activities—for example, "Does the activity foster helpfulness?" and "Does the activity ensure that all families can participate fairly regardless of economics, English proficiency, etc.?"

## Including Teachers and Staff

Everyone likes to know what is going on, how they can participate, and what will be expected of them—people like to be included and informed. This is especially true when activities grow out of classroom work or lead to a change in scheduling for the entire school. For example, if you decide to begin the year with the activity People Who Make It Work, teachers and staff need to be informed about the activity and asked to contribute their ideas for the classroom component. If the school is about to do a Schoolwide Mural, the art teacher, custodial staff, and teachers all need to agree to their part in making it happen.

Consider the following suggestions in your efforts to invite, inform, and involve teachers and staff people from the start:

- Present the proposed activity at a staff meeting; let teachers know why you are planning the activity and how they will be asked to participate (you might want to distribute copies of the activity description).
- Encourage teachers to ask questions, make suggestions, and add new ideas; make sure that teachers support the activity.
- If the activity involves classroom work, hand out copies of the Suggestions for Teachers page for that activity and lead a discussion about how teachers might use or modify the suggestions to meet their students' needs.
- Talk about your plan to communicate with families, and ask for feedback.
- Send a special memo inviting nonteaching staff members to participate in the activity; ask one member of the Coordinating Team to volunteer as the liaison to these staff members all year.
- Consider matching nonteaching staff members to specific classrooms which they can join for schoolwide community-building activities throughout the year.

## Reaching Out to Parents and Families

Just as teachers and staff need to be invited to participate in schoolwide activities, so do parents and families. Here are a few general suggestions to start with; also review Strategies for Increasing Parent Involvement which can be found in Part 5.

- Send home a variety of announcements, letters, and reminders (the activities described in this guide include samples of such announcements).
- Translate invitations into the native languages of your students and their parents.
- Ask teachers to "talk up" the schoolwide activities in class and to remind students to bring their families to them.
- Make personal invitations to children in the hallway and on the playground ("Will we see you tonight?").
- Have parents call each other and extend personal invitations.
- Encourage parents to contribute their time, skills, and knowledge to the activities.

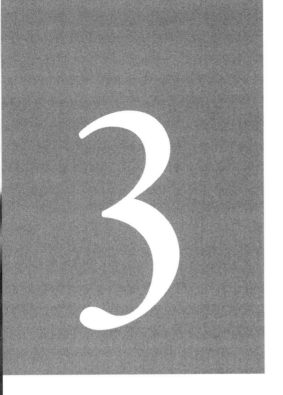

# 3 Activities That Build Community

The activities that follow are designed to help you develop a caring community among the students, families, and staff at your school. We hope they provide you with useful ideas and suggestions for making your community-building efforts successful and fun.

- Getting To Know the People in Our School
- Getting To Know the People in Our Community
- Expanding Our Community
- Sharing What We Learn
- Taking Pride in Our Surroundings

# Getting To Know the People in Our School

**ACTIVITY 1** PEOPLE WHO MAKE IT WORK

**ACTIVITY 2** WELCOMING NEWCOMERS

**ACTIVITY 3** BUDDIES PROGRAM

A caring community is made up of people who come to know and appreciate each other. At school, caring relationships need to be fostered not only in the classroom, but on the playground and throughout the school building as well. Teachers and administrators can help establish such relationships by creating a variety of opportunities throughout the year for children and adults in the school to get to know and care for each other.

ACTIVITY 1

# People Who Make It Work

■ *See also, Suggestions for Teachers, page 85*

In each classroom students interview their teacher and one or more of the non-teaching school staff members and then create vivid displays for a whole-school collage that captures the voices and faces of every adult in the school community. The goal of this activity is to help students get to know the adults they see at school every day—teachers, secretaries, administrators, nurses, librarians, playground monitors, lunchroom staff, classroom aides, social workers, bus drivers, and the custodial staff. The displays can include photographs, drawings, stories, poems, or whatever else fits the interests and ambitions of the collage makers.

## Why This Activity?

The first few weeks of school can be an exciting, but potentially overwhelming, time for children. They are eager to know who their teacher is, who the other adults in the school are, and whether or not they will fit in with the other children. Just as teachers use activities that help children get to know one another in their classroom, this schoolwide project offers children the opportunity to meet and learn about the adults in the school community. As a result, students are likely to feel more comfortable with the adults who work with or around them each day. For staff, this activity offers an opportunity to see themselves as valuable contributors to a whole-community effort to help children grow as learners and as people.

## The Program

### *Getting Ready*

Begin by discussing the proposed project with teachers at a staff meeting, describing its purpose and how they will be asked to participate. Point out that the Coordinating Team will be matching one or two staff people with each classroom, but that the teachers themselves will be responsible for scheduling the interviews (about 20 minutes for each)—including their own. Distribute copies of the suggestions for teachers for this activity, and invite everyone to contribute ideas and suggestions.

Send a memo to nonteaching staff, explaining the activity and requesting their participation (see Sample 1.1 below). Remember to include part-timers, specialists, and consultants. Match each participating adult with a classroom, and notify classroom teachers of these assignments so that they can schedule the interviews. Provide translation as needed.

Make some preliminary decisions about where the school collage might be displayed, the final size of the collage, the size of each classroom's contribution (which should all be of approximately the same size), and the timeline for the project.

### *Classroom Interviews*

Classroom teachers are primarily responsible for managing this aspect of the activity, but students in each classroom should be responsible for deciding how they will conduct the interview and what they will ask. For example, teachers might have students brainstorm categories of information they would like to know about their interview subjects, as well as specific questions for each category; to broaden student thinking about question categories, teachers might also ask students to think about ways to "translate" their interviews into graphically interesting collage pieces. For more details and ideas about what this activity might look like in the classroom, see the suggestions for teachers.

### *Creating the Collage*

In the classrooms, students will create a display about each adult they have interviewed—these displays might include photographs, drawings, stories, quotes, or anything else they want to use to tell the story of the adult and what he or she does in the school community.

Once the class displays are finished, have students from each classroom hang their work and build the collage piece by piece. Once the collage is finished, you may want to create a sign-up schedule for teachers to take their classes to view the collage; you might also want to document the finished piece or invite local media to do so. Remember to take time to acknowledge and celebrate everyone's participation in the project, including your own.

## Adaptations

Based on the students' interviews, create a staff directory featuring a photograph and story about each person and his or her job. If a camera is not available, upper-grade students could interview the staff members, while younger students could make drawings to accompany each person's description.

## Parent Information

Let parents know you are working on a schoolwide collage to help children and school staff members get to know each other. Invite them to visit the school to see the collage. (See Sample 1.2 below).

## Materials & Facilities

- Art supplies
- Camera and film (optional)
- Space to hang the collage

**SAMPLE 1.1** ***LETTER TO THE STAFF***

Dear School Staff Members,

We'd like you to know about our plans for a schoolwide activity called **People Who Make It Work**, and to invite your participation—in fact, we can't do this activity without you!

As part of our effort to build our schoolwide sense of community, we want to "introduce" students to all the teachers and staff members in the school. To do this, the students in each class will interview their teacher and at least one other adult in the school. They will make a display to show what they learned about each person they interviewed, and then all the class displays will be combined into a whole-school collage. This way, students can look at the collage and get to know the many adults they see at school every day in other classrooms, the library, the lunchroom, the office, on the playground, and on the bus.

We guarantee this will be fun for everyone, and we hope you'll agree to participate. Also, we'd love to hear your ideas, suggestions, or questions. Please let us know by returning the form below to our mailbox in the Main Office. Thanks!

---

Name:
Room/Phone:

☐ Yes, I'd like to participate. Please match me with a classroom and have the teacher contact me.
☐ No, I'm unable to participate.
☐ I have questions! Please have someone from the Coordinating Team contact me.

Ideas & Suggestions ______________________________________________

________________________________________________________________

## SAMPLE 1.2 *LETTER TO FAMILIES*

Dear Family Members and Family Friends,

As part of our efforts to build a stronger school community, the children at (NAME) School have been participating in a schoolwide effort called **People Who Make It Work**. For this activity, students have interviewed the adults in the school and now are creating a schoolwide collage to show what they learned from their interviews.

The collage features the members of our school staff, including teachers, classroom aides, playground monitors, custodians, cafeteria staff, administrators—all the adults who make our school work.

The collage will be displayed in the (LOCATION) from (DATE) to (DATE). We hope you'll visit the school to see the collage and learn more about the adults in our school community and what they do here!

ACTIVITY 2

# Welcoming Newcomers

■ *See also, Suggestions for Teachers, page 87*

This activity helps new students, especially those who arrive midyear, to feel a part of their new school community. A group of students representing their respective classrooms—the "Welcomers Committee"—creates the plan for introducing new students to their school, whether through a partner program, a school tour, a school community information packet, or a combination of ideas. When left to design and be responsible for their own ways to welcome new students, children react generously, calling on their own understanding of the difficulties of entering a new situation.

## Why This Activity?

It's hard to be "the new kid," and an ongoing program that welcomes new students can ease each child's entry into the school community. This activity also encourages all students to think about ways to welcome newcomers, fosters their sense of pride in their school, and allows a cross-age group of students to represent their classmates and assume a leadership role. By engaging in such a peer-helping situation, both the "welcomers" and the newcomers can experience the values of caring, helping, and taking responsibility for others. Welcoming Newcomers can also provide an important service for visitors, such as families who are considering sending their children to the school, teachers from other schools, student teachers, district personnel, and any other guests.

## The Program

### *Getting Ready*

Invite teachers' suggestions about how to set a welcoming tone throughout the school, what individual classrooms might do, and how students might be chosen or nominated for the Welcomers Committee. Make some decisions about how the committee will be assembled (for example, two students from each classroom sit on the committee), who will act as the adult advisor, and how time will be scheduled for this group to work together.

### *Classroom Activities*

Encourage teachers to plan some climate-building activities early in the year that focus on how it feels to be new, what people can do to make newcomers feel more comfortable, and what students would like newcomers to know about their school community. As a class, students could brainstorm ideas for what the Welcomers Committee might plan and then select students to represent their class on the committee. For additional classroom strategies, see the suggestions for teachers.

### *Welcomers Committee*

With the guidance of an adult advisor, students on this committee draw upon their recent classroom discussions to decide how they would like to welcome new students to the school. Once students design their welcoming program, the advisor should establish a process for the main office to inform the committee of when a new student or visitor is about to arrive. The advisor should also schedule regular (not necessarily frequent) meetings with the committee so that members can reflect upon their experiences and learn together. For example, each meeting might begin with an opportunity for students to talk about the following: What is going well? Are there any difficulties? Are there any new ideas or suggestions?

Here are a few possibilities the committee might want to consider as they shape the program:

- **Partner Program.** The Welcomers Committee finds students to act as classroom partners for newcomers during the new students' first week in school. The partner helps by introducing the new student to other children and by explaining where things are, who the teachers are, and basic classroom routines and expectations. The partner also makes sure that the new student is included in lunch and recess groups. If the newcomer student is in the lower grades, the welcomers might invite an upper-grade student to spend time with the new student as well.

- **School Tour.** Members of the Welcomers Committee conduct a school tour for newcomers and visitors, during which they show the physical layout of the school building and grounds, describe what they are learning, share their thoughts about what makes the school community a special place, and answer questions. Although they will need to work with the advisor, students are encouraged to work cooperatively to design the tour themselves, create a loose script, and lead tours in pairs or trios.

- **School Packet.** The Welcomers Committee develops an information packet or folder to introduce newcomers and visitors to the school. For example, such packets can include information about the school schedule, a schoolwide calendar, a map, a list of clubs and activities, photos, a statement of welcome from the PTA or principal, and information about special programs at the school. Encourage students also to include a sampling of student poems, drawings, and personal observations in the packet.

- **Getting To Know You Bulletin Board.** Students prepare a monthly Getting to Know You bulletin board that features new students, teachers, or other school staff members. The board could include photographs, artwork, and information about each person.

## Adaptations

This program could be part of a larger student council program in which students take on leadership and decision-making roles within the school and in the wider community.

If your school has access to videotaping and editing equipment, have students create a video about their school community that features interviews with students, staff, and parents, as well as footage of classroom activities, schoolwide events, and original student work.

## Materials & Facilities

- A collection of existing materials about the school for the committee to consider including in the School Packet
- Supplies for students to create their own inserts for the packet
- Camera and film, a bulletin board, and miscellaneous art supplies for students to create the Getting to Know You displays

## Parent Information

Send a note home to newcomers' parents, letting them know how their child is being welcomed into the school community. Include the name of their child's partner, as well as any requests for photographs or other materials for a Getting to Know You bulletin board.

## Outside Resources

Consider partnering with a local television station, public relations company, or parent volunteer to produce a video about the school community.

ACTIVITY 3

# Buddies Program

■ ***See also, Suggestions for Teachers, page 89***

Every student in the school is matched with an older or younger "buddy" for a variety of activities that allow the two children to develop a special kind of friendship—one that is outside of the usual classroom, family, and neighborhood circles. Activities are chosen for their academic and social value and are carefully planned to ensure that buddies get to know one another, build trust, and feel comfortable learning together. For more ideas about implementing a buddies program, please see the Cross-Age Buddies Activity Book, one of the four components of the CSC program.

## Why This Activity?

The Buddies Program helps break down the barriers that often exist in age-graded school settings, and as a result teachers often see less teasing and more spontaneous helpful behavior among children of all ages. Older students benefit by taking the role of a responsible, caring friend and experiencing themselves as someone with much to offer others. Younger students benefit from the extra attention they receive and the positive role model their buddy presents.

## The Program

### *Getting Ready*

Because the Buddies Program relies heavily on teachers to orchestrate it, make sure that teachers are committed to trying it out in their classrooms and that they have the support and materials needed to make it run smoothly. We recommend that members of the Coordinating Team spend some time at a staff meeting—at least one half hour—explaining the program to teachers, providing them with resources, and inviting them to add their own ideas and suggestions.

Encourage teachers to plan a variety of activities that help children get to know their buddies, learn with their buddies, share special times together, and reflect on their experiences together. Present a framework to teachers for how they might structure a year-long program of buddy experiences, based on the ideas that appear in the suggestions for teachers.

The ideas are grouped into the following three categories:

- **Getting-To-Know-You Activities.** These help students get to know the children in their buddy classroom; for example, *Draw Your Buddy* has children interview each other and draw their impressions, and *Special Stories* has children share mementos and objects of personal significance.
- **Ongoing Activities.** These include any activities that continue throughout the school year, thereby building and deepening students' buddy relationship. Such activities include *Journals*, in which each child records his or her buddy experiences, thoughts, and feelings; classroom *Bulletin Boards* that feature photographs or other displays of each buddy pair; a *Pen Pal* mailbox for buddies to send letters to each other; *Special Times*, when older buddies accompany younger ones to assemblies, events, or other school activities; and a variety of *Academic Activities*, such as peer teaching, tutoring, reading aloud, cooperative projects, or presentations for a buddy class.
- **End-of-the-Year Activities.** These give buddies a chance to reflect together on the things they have done throughout the year and to thank each other. *Reviewing the Year*, for example, asks buddies to choose a favorite activity to illustrate and write about together; and *Expressing Appreciation* invites each class to make a special project for their buddy class to thank them for being buddies.

### *Matching Buddy Classrooms*

Once teachers agree to participate in the Buddies Program, the Coordinating Team will need to work with them to make sure that all classrooms are partnered and that upper-grade classrooms are paired with lower-grade classrooms. Encourage teachers to choose their own partners. Some schools have been successful by pairing kindergartners with third-graders, first-graders with fourth-graders, and second-graders with fifth-graders. Leave it up to the teachers of paired classes to work together to match the student buddies.

### *Ongoing Support for Teachers*

Members of the Coordinating Team can support teachers by assisting them with any special needs that arise from the program and by hosting informal meetings a few times throughout the year to give teachers an opportunity to talk about the Buddies Program—what's working well, what's not working well, what ideas people might have for other buddy activities, and so on.

## Adaptations

Consider ways to combine the Buddies Program with other schoolwide activities—for example, have buddies pair up and work together on the school mural, school community garden, or any other community-building activity. You might also encourage teachers to solicit students' ideas and engage students in a whole-class decision-making process to brainstorm and choose activities they might enjoy doing with their buddy class.

## Parent Information

Let parents know about the Buddies Program, and encourage them to discuss it with their children at home (see Sample 3.1 below).

## Materials & Facilities

- Art supplies
- Camera (optional)
- Bulletin boards

## SAMPLE 3.1 *LETTER TO FAMILIES*

Dear Family Members and Family Friends,

This year at (NAME) School we're making an extra effort to build a stronger sense of community, to create a place where children feel comfortable and cared for. As a start, we've been thinking about ways to help children get to know more of the other children at school.

Next week we're going to start a **Buddies Program**. Each classroom will be matched with another classroom in the school, and each child will be assigned a "buddy" from the other class. Children in grades K–2 will be matched with an older buddy, and children in grades 3–5 will be matched with a younger buddy. Our goal is to help older children experience being responsible, caring friends and to help the younger children feel comfortable and cared for at school.

Activities will be arranged so that buddy "pairs" can get to know one another and develop friendships. Throughout the year, children will continue to work with their buddies on special projects and academic activities.

We hope you will take a few minutes next week to ask your child about his or her buddy and what it's like to have an older or younger friend. Thanks . . . and please let us know how your child is enjoying having a special buddy!

# Getting To Know the People in Our Community

**ACTIVITY 4** FAMILY HERITAGE MUSEUM

**ACTIVITY 5** FAMILY PROJECTS FAIR

**ACTIVITY 6** GRANDPERSONS GATHERING

One of the important ways that adults and children in a school come to know and understand each other better is by knowing more about each other's families. Although every activity that welcomes families to school is an opportunity to build schoolwide community, some activities can be structured specifically to focus on families by giving family members a chance to share something special about their heritage, their interests, or their history.

ACTIVITY 4

# Family Heritage Museum

■ *See also, Suggestions for Teachers, page 92*

Students and staff members contribute to a schoolwide display of information and artifacts that tell something about their own family heritage. At home, children and parents decide on their family's contribution to the museum by talking, telling stories, looking at photographs, and investigating their family's history together. This activity can also be a culminating event for individual classroom studies of family history and cultural heritage.

---

## Why This Activity?

The creation of a schoolwide Family Heritage Museum is an enjoyable way for children and parents to celebrate their family background, honor their life experiences, and share pride in their heritage. School staff members are also encouraged to contribute to the museum, so that everyone learns about everyone else's unique background and gains a deeper appreciation for the diversity within the school community.

## The Program

### *Getting Ready*

Introduce the program to teachers and invite them to spend some time in their classroom focusing on family heritage during the month before the museum opens. Consider distributing copies of the suggestions for teachers and facilitating a discussion about incorporating these and other activities in classroom learning. Share the Coordinating Team's plans for the museum itself, and invite feedback.

### *Creating the Family Heritage Museum*

Invite students, parents, teachers, and school staff members to contribute family history stories or artifacts (for example, old family photos, traditional clothing, maps, passports, scrapbooks, letters, certificates, and so on) to the Family Heritage Museum. The museum could be set up in the gymnasium, library, or a section of each classroom, and arranging the museum display could be the responsibility of upper-grade students, a particular class, or a cross-age student committee with parent and teacher advisors. If display space is limited or if there are concerns about some families' limited ability to participate, consider asking each family to bring only one artifact.

### *Community Mapping*

Schools involved in CDP have shown us that welcoming families as they walk in the door of the school is one of the most important components of any schoolwide activity. If the principal and a few students are at the door greeting children, parents, and other guests, everyone is likely to feel welcome and more comfortable being at the school. For this particular event, as families enter the building and are greeted, they could be introduced to Community Mapping, a way to show each family's origin and the migration patterns for the entire community: on a huge map of the world, have families place push pins of a particular color on their ancestral countries or states, and push pins of another color on places where their generation has lived. By the end of the evening, the map will be covered with markings that show both diverse and common experiences within the school.

## Adaptations

There are countless classroom and whole-school activities that can be integrated into an extended study of family history and cultural heritage; for a few ideas, see the suggestions for teachers.

A possible adaptation for the museum opening event would be to make time for families to meet together in small groups to learn about each other's displays. Teachers could facilitate these small-group discussions.

Another adaptation would be to initiate a Speakers Series, inviting family members or older adults in the community to visit the school and share stories from their life or folktales that reflect their cultural heritage. (See also Activity 6: Grandpersons Gathering.)

## Parent Information

Three separate notices about the Family Heritage Museum should be sent home (see samples below). The first should be a general announcement that explains the purpose of the museum, encourages families to participate, and offers ideas about how they might contribute to the effort. The second notice could include suggestions about what might be included in a display, as well as specific information about the time, date, and place of the event; this notice should also encourage parents to attend the event, not just drop off their children. Send a third notice a few days before the event as a final reminder.

## Staff Information

Teachers and nonteaching staff members should receive a formal invitation to contribute to the museum (see Sample 4.4 below).

## Things to Consider

It is important to design these activities in a way that invites all families to participate equally and at the same time. For example, we strongly advise against a series of events that focuses first on one cultural group or geographic area, then on another, and so forth.

Some students may find it difficult or impossible to involve their parents or family in this activity. Special care will need to be taken to find ways for these students to participate meaningfully.

## Materials & Facilities

- Museum set-up, including tables, bulletin boards, posters, tape, signs
- Large world map and push pins in two colors for the Community Mapping activity

### SAMPLE 4.1 *LETTER TO FAMILIES*

Dear Family Members and Family Friends,

As part of learning more about the people in our school community, we are sponsoring a schoolwide **Family Heritage Museum** during the week of (DATE).

Your child will be asking you for something to display in the museum, such as a photograph, family tree, map, piece of clothing, diary, or any other object that tells something about your family heritage and life experiences. Please write a description of what the object is and why you chose it.

Also, rather than sending an artifact to display, you could instead have your child interview you about your family or family heritage. Maybe you'd like to tell a favorite family story or joke or share a favorite story from when you were growing up. Your child can then write or draw about one of the family stories you tell. However you decide to contribute, feel free to involve your whole family in sharing family stories and creating the display.

Next week you will receive more information about how to participate and when to visit our Family Heritage Museum. Until then, think about what you might like to share with your child and our school community!

## SAMPLE 4.2 *FOLLOW-UP LETTER TO FAMILIES*

Dear Family Members and Family Friends,

As you know, we will be sponsoring a schoolwide **Family Heritage Museum** during the week of (DATE). This letter tells you more about how your family can participate.

- **To Create a Family Display**
  Decide as a family what you would like to display in the museum. Feel free to include photographs, a family heirloom, a story, illustration, or any other item that tells others something about your family and its history. Make sure that you and your child include a brief description of your display and why you chose it. All displays should be brought to school by the end of the day on (DATE), and they can be brought home on (DATE). (Remember to put your name on any items in your display.)
- **Family Heritage Museum Opening Night**
  We hope you and your family will be able to join us for the opening of the Family Heritage Museum on (DATE) from (TIMES) at (NAME) School. This is an important community event for students and their parents, so please make every effort to accompany your child; do not drop off children at the event unattended.

We look forward to seeing you there!

### SAMPLE 4.3 *REMINDER LETTER*

REMINDER!

This is to remind you that the **Family Heritage Museum** opens next week! Bring your display to school on (DATE) between (TIME) and (TIME), and join us for the opening of the Museum at (TIME).

We look forward to seeing you next (DAY).

### SAMPLE 4.4 *LETTER TO THE STAFF*

Dear School Staff Members,

As part of learning more about the people in our school community, we are sponsoring a schoolwide Family Heritage Museum during the week of (DATE).

We'd like you to bring something to display in the museum, such as a photograph, family tree, map, piece of clothing, diary, or any other object that tells something about your family heritage and life experiences. Please write a description of what the object is and why you chose it. Or, you could write about or illustrate a favorite family story or event. Feel free to involve your whole family in sharing family stories and creating the display.

All displays should be brought to school by the end of the day on (DATE), and they can be brought home on (DATE). (Remember to put your name on any items in your display.)

We hope you and your family will be able to join us for the opening of the Family Heritage Museum on (DATE) from (TIMES) at (NAME) School. This is an important community event for all of you, so please make every effort to contribute to the museum and attend the opening.

We look forward to seeing you there!

ACTIVITY 5

# Family Projects Fair

■ *See also, Suggestions for Teachers, page 94*

A Family Projects Fair begins with families deciding on a cooperative project to do at home—for example, they might document a project that they work on together, such as planting a garden; create a project such as a science experiment or model; or make a display about a family interest, such as baseball or rock collecting. The emphasis should be on the process of working together as a family, rather than on the resulting "product." Families then show their projects at school for the Family Projects Fair, during which they can both explain their work to other families in the school community and learn from the other families' projects.

---

## Why This Activity?

By collaborating on a project at home, parents and children get a chance to explore new ideas and create something together. The activity includes practical suggestions for parents on how to work on this project with their children, thereby reinforcing at home the cooperative learning strategies their children are practicing at school. Finally, the fair offers a safe, noncompetitive environment for parents and children to learn together and enjoy participating in their school community.

## The Program

### *Getting Ready*

Because the Family Projects Fair is a culmination of work that parents and children have done together at home, it requires relatively little classroom and school time other than on-site preparations for the fair itself. Because this activity is so family directed, however, it is very important that families understand the instructions and rationale for the fair. Specifically, make sure that parents and children understand that the point of this project is the cooperative work, not the product, and offer them several creative suggestions for projects to think about in advance. At a staff meeting, discuss how teachers can help convey the spirit and purpose of this activity. Distribute the suggestions for teachers and invite feedback.

### *Classroom Activities*

As noted in the suggestions for teachers, we recommend that each teacher introduce the Family Projects Fair in class, brainstorming with students the kinds of projects they could create with parents or other family members at home. Students can then add their brainstorming ideas to the list of suggestions on Sample 5.1 below.

### *Suggestions for Parents*

In order to begin their projects, families will first need a few suggestions to help them choose an idea. In the sample letters that follow, we've included a list of possible activities and some guidelines about how to make a cooperative decision about the project they'd like to work on, as well as some ideas on how to make the process truly cooperative. Again, the letter to families should emphasize the importance of families thinking, discussing, exploring, and creating together.

### *Family Projects Fair*

On the evening of the event, families can set up their projects an hour before the fair. "Like" projects can be organized together (for example, science, art, family heritage), or projects can be mixed randomly or in classroom groups. Make sure that families receive a warm welcome as they come in, and encourage them to view other family displays as well as to describe their project to others. (Besides this opening night event, also consider having classrooms take turns visiting the fair for a closer look at the displays.)

## Adaptations

Offer a Family Projects Workshop for families interested in learning more about working on projects together at home. Ask teachers and parents with special skills or interests to lead workshops about them—for example, bookmaking, weaving, hands-on science projects, and so on.

Consider a Thematic Projects Fair about a particular subject area or schoolwide theme that is being introduced across the curriculum. For example, a school focusing on the topic of migration or "people of America" could invite families to work on projects related to this theme.

## Parent Information

Three separate notices should be sent home about the Family Projects Fair (see samples below). The first should give the date of the event, explain its purpose, and provide guidelines for cooperatively choosing and working on a project. The second should remind families about the event and include a form for them to fill out and return to school, preliminarily describing their cooperative projects (which they can always change if they'd like). The third notice should provide details about where and when families can set up their projects and attend the fair.

## Things to Consider

Ideally, the first letter to families should be sent home after classes have had a chance to discuss the activity and brainstorm ideas for creative projects. Teachers also might encourage their students to add to the letters any ideas from their class brainstorming activity.

As with any family activity, some students may not have family members willing or able to work with them. If this is the case for many students, you might not want to attempt this activity; if this is true for relatively few students, consider helping them find another supportive person or group to work with on a cooperative project.

## Materials & Facilities

- Tables set up in a large room to accommodate all projects and traffic
- Access to electrical outlets or water, if any registered projects require this

## Outside Resources

Consider the strengths and talents of parents in the school community, some of whom may be able to offer creative suggestions or workshops for others.

**SAMPLE 5.1** ***LETTER TO FAMILIES***

Dear Family Members and Family Friends,

Have you ever thought of creating an invention? Have you always wanted to make a book about your family's history? Have you ever tried to sprout mung beans in wet paper towels? If questions like these spark your family's interest in exploring and discovering together, then the **Family Projects Fair** is for you!

On (DATE), our school will open its doors to the Family Projects Fair, a schoolwide celebration of the creative projects that families work on together. We invite the families in our school community to explore a topic at home together and then share what you have learned with the rest of us.

If your family can't decide what kind of project to do, think about something you've been interested in working on, but haven't had the time for. Or think of a question that makes your family curious, and make a display that answers that question. Try to think of a display that might fit on a table or in a small floor space. Here are some ideas:

- Create a family book or story
- Make a musical instrument
- Build a solar system
- Make up a game
- Create a video about your family
- Grow crystals
- Build a 3-dimensional map
- Make masks for the whole family
- Plan an outing to someplace new
- Rate television programs using a graph
- Make a timeline of your life as a family
- Create a model, diorama, or quilt
- What are the sounds of our neighborhood?
- What foods do pigeons like best?

Please remember that the goal of this project is to enjoy working cooperatively, not to create the "best" product, so we've enclosed a list of suggestions for helping the work go smoothly. Next week, additional information and registration forms will be sent home. We encourage you to start thinking about your family's project now—and have fun!

## SAMPLE 5.2 *ENCLOSURE FOR LETTER TO FAMILIES*

Five Suggestions for Choosing and Organizing a Cooperative Family Project

- **Choose a project that will be fun for everyone, and enjoy yourselves!**
- **When trying to decide on a topic, think about how you like to spend your free time as a family.** Tips: What do you enjoy doing together? Is there anything you would like to fix or change in the house or apartment? Is there a cause your family cares about? Is there anything on the list of topics that particularly interests you?
- **Make as many joint decisions as possible.** Tips: Encourage everyone to voice an opinion and add his or her thoughts; make it clear from the beginning that there are no wrong or "dumb" answers; avoid voting.
- **After agreeing on your project, list the things that need to be done to finish the project and have family members choose jobs.** Tips: Make sure everyone has jobs they can handle; talk about the tasks that are involved in doing your chosen topic before jobs are divided; pair younger children with an adult or a willing older sibling so they can be helpers on difficult tasks.
- **Discuss the activity together.** Tips: Ask questions with many possible responses (for example, "What do you like best about our project?" or "What do you think we should do next?"); set time aside to discuss how the work is going and how you are feeling.

## SAMPLE 5.3 FOLLOW-UP LETTER AND REGISTRATION

Dear Family Members and Family Friends,

As you know, you are invited to participate in the **Family Projects Fair**, to be held on (DATE) at (TIME) in the (LOCATION).

We'd like to get an idea of how many families plan to participate and the types of projects that will be displayed. Please complete the form below and return it to your child's teacher by (DATE). But don't worry if your project idea changes along the way . . . that's part of the fun!

---

PLEASE RETURN TO YOUR CHILD'S TEACHER BY (DATE)

Name: ______________________________

Teacher's name: ______________________________

☐ Our cooperative project for the Family Projects Fair will be:

______________________________

______________________________

☐ We are still deciding what our project will be.

☐ Help! We need an idea!

☐ We will need special accommodations for our project:

___ wall space

___ electrical hook-up

___ water supply

___ other ______________________________

☐ Our family will not be creating a cooperative project, but we know that we are welcome to come to the fair and enjoy the exhibits.

## SAMPLE 5.4 *FINAL DETAILS*

Dear Family Members and Family Friends,

This is a reminder that the **Family Projects Fair** will be held next week in the school (LOCATION) on (DATE). If you haven't already let us know of anything special you need to display your project, please return the form below now.

Your family has display space # _________ at the fair. When you come to set up your project, look for your number on one of the tables or wall areas. Projects may be assembled during the hour before the fair opens from (TIME) to (TIME).

The fair will be open for family viewing between (TIME) and (TIME) p.m., and classes will visit the fair again the next day during school. We ask that families dismantle their projects and remove them by (DATE).

We look forward to seeing you there!

---

PLEASE RETURN TO YOUR CHILD'S TEACHER BY (DATE)

Name: ____________________________________________

Teacher's name: ____________________________________

Display space # _____________________________________

☐ We will need special accommodations for our project:

___ wall space

___ electrical hook-up

___ water supply

___ other ___________________________________________

ACTIVITY 6

# Grandpersons Gathering

■ *See also, Suggestions for Teachers, page 96*

Grandpersons Gathering is a time for students to celebrate a special relationship they have with a grandparent or other adult "grandperson." Students invite a grandparent or an older friend, neighbor, or relative to be their guest at school for an afternoon. Various activities foster an open exchange between children and the visitors, introduce the grandpersons to the school community, and help teachers and staff members learn more about the significant adults in children's lives.

## Why This Activity?

Because grandparents and other older people can play such a meaningful role in children's lives, it is important for them to be included in the children's school community. At the same time, children without grandparents or grandpersons available for this activity can be invited into a special relationship of "sharing" a grandperson.

## The Program

### *Getting Ready*

Introduce the idea of Grandpersons Gathering to teachers at a staff meeting and invite everyone to participate. Lead a discussion about how the afternoon might take shape, distribute copies of the suggestions for teachers, and invite teachers' ideas about possible schoolwide or classroom activities. Send a memo to nonteaching staff members inviting them to join a classroom and perhaps act as an "honorary grandperson" for the event; match each interested staff member with a class (see Sample 6.3 below).

### *Inviting Grandpersons*

Have students invite grandparents or another older adult such as a neighbor, friend, or relative; parents should be encouraged to help their children make these arrangements (see Sample 6.1 below). It should also be made clear to students that they will be expected to share their visiting grandperson with any children who are unable to have grandpersons visit. Grandpersons are also free to visit more than one classroom if they have more than one grandchild at school.

### *Welcoming Grandpersons*

Arrange for a small group of students to act as a welcoming committee that greets the grandpersons as they arrive at school, makes name tags for them, invites them to sign a guest register, and then escorts them to the classroom they are visiting. After the event, the register can be used to send thank-you letters to the visitors.

### *Classroom-Based Activities*

The classroom activities described in the suggestions for teachers foster personal connections between students and visiting grandpersons through storytelling, interviewing, sharing memorabilia, and working on special projects together. Consider asking teachers to set up centers for these activities throughout the classrooms or school; students could rotate in small groups from center to center, thereby interacting with several grandpersons in a limited time.

### *Schoolwide Activities*

Consider sponsoring a schoolwide assembly that showcases student presentations or storytelling by grandpersons. Another possibility is to sponsor a school picnic so that children and grandpersons have time to enjoy being together in a relaxed environment; some schools plan games, music, and dancing during this part of the visit.

## Parent Information

Parents should receive two notices (see samples below). The first should explain the purpose of the event and encourage parents to help their children participate; a reminder note should be sent home a week before the event. To establish a welcoming, inclusive tone, and especially to make sure that children feel comfortable inviting significant older adults other than grandparents, we recommend referring to participating adults as "grandpersons" (rather than grandparents) in all announcements and materials.

## Materials & Facilities

- Read-aloud books featuring relationships between children and grandpersons (specific titles are included in the suggestions for teachers)
- Supplies for classroom activities, such as paper, pencils, art materials, video equipment

## SAMPLE 6.1 *LETTER TO FAMILIES*

Dear Family Members and Family Friends,

As part of our ongoing exploration of who's who in our community, we are sponsoring an afternoon event called **Grandpersons Gathering** on (DATE) from (TIME) to (TIME). We are encouraging all students to invite a grandparent or older friend, neighbor, or relative to spend the afternoon with us at school.

If your child would like to invite a grandparent or another grandperson who might be willing to visit our class and share stories, mementos, and a few pleasant hours, please ask the grandperson to complete this form for your child to return to school. Don't worry if your child is unable to invite someone. All children will be included, and those who bring guests will partner with those who do not have a visitor.

---

PLEASE RETURN TO YOUR CHILD'S TEACHER BY (DATE)

Name of Grandperson: ______________________________

Phone: ______________________________

Name of Student: ______________________________

☐ I am willing to bring a special object from my life (such as an old doll or photo album) to tell the class about.

______________________________

______________________________

☐ I am willing to bring something I have created (such as a sweater, birdhouse, or poem) and tell the class about making it.

______________________________

______________________________

☐ I am willing to be interviewed by the children.

## SAMPLE 6.2 *REMINDER TO FAMILIES*

REMINDER!

Don't forget that on (DATE) we are hosting a **Grandpersons Gathering** at (NAME) School from (TIME) to (TIME). We are looking forward to an enriching and fun afternoon with our grandpersons and other friends.

If you would like to invite a grandperson, please remember to return the questionnaire we recently sent home as soon as possible. We'd like to know in advance how many grandpersons will be with us, but last-minute visitors are more than welcome.

Thanks . . . and parents are welcome, too!

## SAMPLE 6.3 *LETTER TO THE STAFF*

Dear School Staff Members,

As part of our ongoing exploration of who's who in our community, we are sponsoring a **Grandpersons Gathering** on (DATE) from (TIME) to (TIME). We are encouraging all students to invite a grandparent or older friend, neighbor, or relative to spend the afternoon with us at school.

We'd like to extend an invitation as well to all staff members who are willing to act as "honorary grandpersons" in one of our classrooms. Please let us know if you are interested and what times you are available. We hope you'll join us!

PLEASE RETURN TO (NAME), (ROOM OR PHONE) BY (DATE)

________________________________________

NAME OF STAFF PERSON

________________________________________

SCHOOL LOCATION OR PHONE

________________________________________

ANY PARTICULAR CLASS YOU WOULD LIKE TO VISIT

# Expanding Our Community

**ACTIVITY 7** ADOPT-A-FAMILY

**ACTIVITY 8** WORKING FOR A CAUSE

Helping children grow up to be caring and generous members of the world community can be one of the most satisfying aspects of working in a caring school. The values and norms that children experience and practice as members of a school community give them a platform from which to expand their notion of community—to include people who may be very different from them, who may live far away from them, and whom they may never have a chance to know personally.

ACTIVITY 7

# Adopt-a-Family

■ *See also, Suggestions for Teachers, page 100*

Adopt-a-Family allows the entire school community to think about and attend to the needs of others. In collaboration with a local social service agency, each classroom is matched with a family in need of such basic items as clothes, food, books, and toys. Each class then takes responsibility for deciding how to assist this family. Although schools typically initiate this program during the holiday season, classrooms often choose to continue providing support for their family throughout the year.

---

## Why This Activity?

This activity promotes the values of caring about and helping others. Students learn that by being thoughtful and working together as a caring community, they can make a real difference in the lives of others; they also have an opportunity to reflect on their own lives and see that even while they may face their own challenges, they are still able to care for others. Parents are kept informed about Adopt-a-Family activities, making both the classroom and the home a forum for discussing the values of caring, helping, and taking responsibility.

## The Program

Each school will shape its Adopt-a-Family program in its own way, but the universal goal should be to create an opportunity for all students, regardless of their own financial situation, to experience the value of helping others and to learn that everyone has something to give.

### *Getting Ready*

At a staff meeting, present Adopt-a-Family to teachers and staff and invite their participation. Lead a discussion about the benefits of this activity, the socioeconomic conditions in your particular school community, and potential problems that could arise (see Things to Consider below). Make sure that everyone is in agreement about how Adopt-a-Family will be structured and communicated to both parents and students.

### *Collaboration with a Community Agency*

Your school may already have a relationship with a local social service agency or the Department of Social Services. If not, initiate contact with an appropriate agency—one that has the capacity to provide confidential information about the needs of a number of families and to distribute the school's gifts to the adopted families. (If you are unable to locate the appropriate agency, contact the United Way in your area for assistance.)

One person from the Coordinating Team should serve as the liaison to this agency, which can provide background information about each family (such as the age and gender of family members, their clothing and shoe sizes, their special interests or hobbies, and so on). Match each classroom with a family, and give this background information to the teacher to share with students (the names of the "adopted" families, of course, must remain confidential).

### *Classroom Activities*

Teacher and students discuss the importance of helping and thinking of others, and then students decide how their class would like to support their newly adopted family. (For more details and ideas about the classroom component of this activity, see the suggestions for teachers.)

### *Helping as a School Community*

A graphic way to demonstrate and celebrate the value of helping others is to have all the classes and nonteaching staff bring their gifts to a central place in the school where everyone can see the collective impact they have when they work together. This also may be an opportune time to schedule a schoolwide assembly or student presentation about the value of taking responsibility in one's community and helping others.

Transporting the collected gifts to the social service agency for delivery to each family may require a small caravan of volunteer drivers.

## Adaptations

If Adopt-a-Family is not feasible in your community, consider adopting a nursing home, the children's wing of a local hospital, or a shelter for homeless families. A variety of international programs also enable schools to develop partnerships with others in need throughout the world.

If your school community is composed primarily of needy families, you may want to focus on the theme that we all have needs and we all have something to share. You could sponsor an Extending Our Families service to which families contribute items they no longer need or skills they have to offer.

## Parent Information

It's important to let parents know about any Adopt-a-Family program, so send them a notice that describes the program and encourages them to participate with their children either by discussing the program, choosing gifts, or making a gift together as a family. Parents should understand that the emphasis is on thinking about and helping others in whatever way possible; in affluent communities, you may need to strongly discourage expensive gift-giving and the competition it might engender in the classroom. In needy communities, you may want to acknowledge in your letter to families that you recognize their circumstances and are asking for only that which they can truly spare. Send a second notice to let parents know specifically what their child's class has agreed on as their project, and how a parent might help; then send a final reminder notice a week before the donation deadline (see samples below). Afterwards, or throughout the year if this is an ongoing activity, you might want to send another letter to let parents know how much you accomplished as a school community.

## Things to Consider

The main goal of this activity is to involve everyone in contributing to the effort while avoiding competition or comparisons. For example, some schools that have experimented with the Adopt-a-Family program over the years encourage students to bring new or used items that are wrapped and labeled, so as to avoid comparisons. Other schools establish a maximum contribution to buy a gift (such as one dollar); they also encourage parents to provide ways for their children to earn any money they contribute to the program.

This activity works best in a school community where families are in fairly similar economic conditions, whether affluent, average, or modest. If your school serves two distinct communities with marked economic differences, we recommend using Activity 8: Working for a Cause instead.

## Materials & Facilities

- A designated collection area in each classroom
- Art supplies to make cards, projects, wrapping paper, etc.
- Large boxes for transporting the collected gifts
- Volunteers to drive the collected gifts to the cooperating social service agency

## SAMPLE 7.1 LETTER TO FAMILIES

Dear Family Members and Family Friends,

As part of our schoolwide effort to help others, classes at (NAME) School will be participating in an **Adopt-a-Family** program this year.

Beginning in (MONTH), each class will be matched with a family that needs such basic items as food, clothing, toys, and books. The arrangements will be made by (AGENCY), and all family names will be kept confidential. Each class will then decide how to help its adopted family. We might send them handmade cards or gifts, clothing (new and used), food for a holiday meal, or a gift that we purchase together.

Of course, we need your help! Our goal is to enable children to work together to help others, not to see who can contribute the most expensive gift. Please don't let your child worry about who's giving the best gift or the most money. Instead, please stress the importance of helping others in whatever way we are able. We will send some ideas about how you might participate once your child's class has decided what it wants to do to help its adopted family.

We encourage you to build on the momentum we're creating at school and make Adopt-a-Family a project for your whole family!

## SAMPLE 7.2 FOLLOW-UP LETTER TO FAMILIES

Dear Family Members and Family Friends,

As you know, our class has been matched with a family in need, as part of the schoolwide **Adopt-a-Family** program this year. We have been working together to make some decisions about how we'd like to help our adopted family.

After considering all of our possibilities, we've decided that we'd like to (SPECIFICALLY DESCRIBE WHAT THE CLASS WILL BE DOING). We encourage you to work with us by helping your child and your family find ways to contribute to this whole-class project.

(provide details for parents, including information about how items should be packaged and labeled.)

Thanks again for helping us make a difference in our community!

## SAMPLE 7.3 *FINAL REMINDER*

REMINDER — One week to go!

Thank you all for your wonderful contributions to our schoolwide **Adopt-a-Family** program. Remember that next (DAY & DATE) is the last day to add donated items to this effort. Please make sure that all items are brought to school no later than (TIME) on (DATE)!

## SAMPLE 7.4 *LETTER TO THE STAFF*

Dear School Staff Members,

As part of our schoolwide effort to help others, classes at (NAME) School will be participating in an **Adopt-a-Family** program this year.

Beginning in (MONTH), each class will be matched with a family that needs such basic items as food, clothing, toys, and books. The arrangements will be made by (AGENCY), and all family names will be kept confidential. Each class will decide how to help its adopted family. Students might send handmade cards or gifts, clothing (new and used), food for a holiday meal, or a gift that is purchased together.

We'd like to invite staff members to contribute to Adopt-a-Family as well. (NAME) will be coordinating all staff contributions, and will be contacting you in the near future. Please let (HER/HIM) know if you'd like to help coordinate staff involvement.

ACTIVITY 8

# Working for a Cause

■ *See also, Suggestions for Teachers, page 102*

Each school picks a "helping" opportunity that interests its students and staff—such as collecting supplies for disaster victims, raising money for a cause, or working together on a community service project such as a toy drive or walk-a-thon. Students apply their considerable energy and ingenuity to a cause that lets them reach out and contribute to the wider community.

---

## Why This Activity?

As is true for Adopt-a-Family, this activity offers students the opportunity to take collective responsibility for helping in their community or in the world. By together deciding how they would like to help with a cause, students are likely to develop an internal commitment to reaching their goal. In the end, they will be able to see that they really can make a difference in the lives of others, their community, and the world—especially when they work together.

## The Program

### *Getting Ready*

Introduce the idea of Working for a Cause at a staff meeting, describing the activity's purpose and value. Distribute the suggestions for teachers and lead a discussion about what cause to address and possible helping activities. Establish a timeline for the project, and notify both families and nonteaching staff members about ways they might participate.

### *Choosing a Cause*

Schools often initiate this activity in response to an event such as a flood, earthquake, or fire, because the disaster relief needs are so evident and pressing. Such efforts usually involve collecting supplies and raising money, and students benefit because their work connects them to victims whose situation might otherwise seem very abstract and remote.

A school needn't wait for a disaster to use this activity, though—you might want to create a list of options for helping in the local community, and then have the staff decide which cause would be the most appropriate focus for the school. Each class can then work on its particular contribution to the schoolwide effort. Another possibility is to make a connection with an agency that addresses an international need, such as hunger or disaster relief. Each class can then decide on ways to address the issue as best fits their grade level and interests.

Several classrooms or the whole school might be involved in a unit of study, such as The Rain Forest, Our City, or The Oceans, and discover things related to their topic of study they could do to make the world better.

### *Ways to Help*

There are countless ways for students and adults to work together to support worthy causes; the suggestions below have been successful at many CDP schools.

- **Collecting Supplies.** Most disaster-relief efforts call for supplies as well as funds, and local social service agencies can identify similar needs in your community as well. Consider initiating a canned food, blanket, or clothing drive to support a disaster-relief or local effort.
- **A Community Service Project.** Students from all grade levels could go out in the community together to work on a specific service project in collaboration with a nearby park, nursing home, SPCA, or other community-based agency. Also consider participating in special events, such as a park or beach clean-up day.

## Parent Information

Let parents know about Working for a Cause activities, and ask for their support both at home and at school. Make it easy for families to become involved in the school's efforts.

## Materials & Facilities

Materials will vary depending on the project your school takes on.

## Outside Resources

Consider approaching large companies and local businesses for matching funds, donations, and sponsorship. Another possibility is to have your entire school join an existing community service or disaster-relief effort sponsored by a local corporation.

# Sharing What We Learn

**ACTIVITY 9** FAMILY READ-A-LOUD

**ACTIVITY 10** FAMILY SCIENCE NIGHT

**ACTIVITY 11** FAMILY MATH

**ACTIVITY 12** FAMILY FILM NIGHT

Research shows that children are more eager to learn and participate at school if they can see that their parents are interested in what they are learning, how they are learning, and what their school experience is like. For many children, though, the trip to school each day can mean an abrupt transition from one world to another; and for a variety of reasons, parents may get no more than a brief glimpse of what their child does at school. One solution is to structure school learning activities in which parents and children participate together and share what they learn.

ACTIVITY 9

# Family Read-Aloud

Family Read-Aloud brings students, families, teachers, and school staff members together in a comfortable environment to enjoy reading. This event helps unite the entire school community around the importance of reading without setting up a competition among students or classes.

## Why This Activity?

In addition to creating an opportunity for family members to experience the joy of reading with each other, Family Read-Aloud is a chance for parents to learn more about the importance of reading with their children and how they can help their children enjoy selecting and reading good books. For students, Family Read-Aloud is an occasion to see that reading is important and exciting for a wide range of the adults in their school community.

## The Program

### *Getting Ready*

Introduce the idea of the Family Read-Aloud at a staff meeting, describing the goal of making reading comfortable and enjoyable for everyone. Gather books for the event, keeping in mind that books—including wordless picture books—should be available for all ages and reading abilities and in all languages children are known to speak at home.

### *Read-Aloud Welcome*

Remember that a warm welcome by the principal and members of the Coordinating Team can be one of the most important parts of a schoolwide activity, so try to greet families and guests as they arrive. Hold the event in a large space such as the library, gymnasium, or cafeteria (you might ask families to bring blankets and pillows to sit on), and begin with a few introductory remarks from the principal about the event. In some schools the principal has introduced the evening by reading aloud a poem or story.

The first time you sponsor a Family Read-Aloud, you might consider following this welcome with a brief orientation (15 minutes) for parents, while students stay in the large room to listen to a story. Have teachers and other staff members meet with parents in small groups to discuss the importance of reading aloud and to provide suggestions on how to read aloud effectively. The group facilitators should model some of these suggestions, such as discussing the book with their children, asking open-ended questions, encouraging children's questions, and sharing their own ideas about a story. Conduct groups for non-English-speaking parents in their native languages.

### *Family Reading*

Distribute tubs of books throughout the room for parents and children to choose from. These tubs should include a variety of books for all reading levels; if your school has a high population of limited or non-English-speaking parents and children, also provide an appropriate selection of books in their home languages. The most exciting part of the evening occurs during the next 20 to 30 minutes, when families gather together around a book. Encourage families to make themselves comfortable and to read in whatever ways they prefer; some parents will read aloud to their children, others will invite their children to read aloud to them, and larger families might split into more than one group so that each child can make a personal selection.

Consider posting a series of open-ended discussion questions, such as the following:

- What did you especially like about this story?
- Has anything like this happened to any of us?
- What questions would we like to ask a character in the story?

### *Family Reflections*

After the read-aloud, invite families to gather in small groups to share their thoughts and feelings about the experience. Place a teacher or parent volunteer with each group to ask a few open-ended questions and help facilitate the discussion: What was it like to read together as a family? What did you like? What surprised you? (Or, if you prefer, bring the whole group back together and conduct a large-group discussion.)

### *Take a Book Home*

Many schools have been successful at promoting reading at home by opening the library at the end of the Family Read-Aloud, or by creating a system for parents to borrow books directly from the tubs.

## Adaptations

Offer families a Multimedia Read-Aloud incorporating art, writing, video, or computers. Begin by having the principal or adult volunteer read a story aloud to everyone. Then have small groups of families meet in individual classrooms for activities such as bookmaking, creating art projects related to the story, writing stories together on the computer, or watching and discussing a short *Reading Rainbow* videotape.

You could also invite a storyteller to present a story prior to the family reading time, or have students perform a story they have prepared in class. Ideally, these presentations should focus on the values and themes of a caring community, such as the importance of fairness, taking responsibility, and helping others.

## Parent Information

Send an invitation to parents, briefly explaining the Family Read-Aloud event (see Sample 9.1 below). Also consider providing parents with an events schedule from the public library, a list of good children's books, tips and strategies for reading at home with their child, the program schedule for *Reading Rainbow*, or any other such material that might promote reading at home.

## Things to Consider

Snacks or hot chocolate are always welcome; some schools have found that delivering a plate of cookies to each small group during the Family Reflections segment adds a pleasant social touch to the families' conversations.

## Materials & Facilities

- Tubs of books gathered from the library or classrooms
- A large-room meeting space
- Microphone (optional)
- Extra blankets or mats (optional)
- Refreshments (optional)

## Outside Resources

Consider partnering with the local public library to sponsor new-card applications and on-the-spot book check-outs.

- *The Read-Aloud Handbook*, by Jim Trelease

## SAMPLE 9.1 *LETTER TO FAMILIES*

Dear Family Members and Family Friends,

Would you like to know more about the importance of reading aloud to your child or how to enjoy a few minutes every day reading together?

We all agree that reading is important, yet there never seems to be enough time to do the reading we'd like. That's why on (DATE), we'll hold a schoolwide **Family Read-Aloud** in the (ROOM). All you have to do is come to the school at (TIME) with your family, and we'll supply the books for a relaxing and informative evening of reading together.

Books will be available in English and (NAME OTHER LANGUAGES), and some will be available for signing out at the end of the evening. Bring a blanket or pillows to sit on, and we'll take care of the rest!

ACTIVITY 10

# Family Science Night

■ *See also, Suggestions for Teachers, page 104*

Family Science Night is a high-involvement "messing around" time for children and their parents. Together, families make their way from classroom to classroom exploring a variety of hands-on science activities that students have created in class during the weeks leading up to the event.

---

## Why This Activity?

Unlike many traditional science fairs, this event allows everyone to experience school as a nonthreatening, friendly place to be, without the tension of competition or the potential risk of failure. Family Science Night lets students take pride in their "workplace" and in their learning—they get to teach their parents, siblings, and other family members about what they are learning, and parents are able to enjoy spending time learning with their children in a relaxed environment. And with hands-on activities in each room, families are able to explore science at a variety of conceptual levels, entertain new ideas, and reinforce what they already know.

## The Program

### *Getting Ready*

Although many of the logistical details for the event can be handled by the Coordinating Team, it's important to have the entire school faculty involved in planning the focus of the science activities. At a staff meeting, lead teachers in a discussion of their existing science emphases for each grade level, and reach agreement on each classroom's focus for Family Science Night. For example, one class may choose to focus on nutrition, another on air pollution, and yet another may decide to study sound or color. Establish a set of parameters for the science stations student groups will create, such as the number of people that can use a station at once and the approximate duration of each activity. Distribute copies of the suggestions for teachers, and encourage teachers to discuss possible activities with their students and to have the class choose activity ideas. Set a timeline for creating a master list of activities students will be working on. Remember to invite nonteaching staff members to attend the fair.

### *Supporting Teachers*

In each classroom, students will develop and set up a variety of science stations around a common theme, and then at the event students will rotate among the stations and assist families as they explore. Keep in mind that planning for and creating these stations will require a lot of teacher participation and classroom time. Offer teachers support and assistance as they and their students prepare for the event.

### *Holding the Event*

Welcome families as they arrive for Family Science Night, and give them a student-created illustrated map that indicates the themes featured in each classroom. Teachers should be available to welcome families to the classrooms and to assist with the demonstrations, especially in lower grades. Classrooms will be filled with parents and children learning together, enjoying themselves, and meeting others.

## Adaptations

Consider a Family Mathematics Fair or Family Arts Festival based on the same principles of noncompetitiveness, cooperation, and inclusion. For additional ideas, see Activity 5: Family Projects Fair and Activity 11: Family Math.

## Parent Information

As classes begin their science projects, send a letter home explaining the purpose and value of the upcoming Family Science Night. Let parents know how much work their children are putting into their contributions to this event and how important it is to attend with their children. Send a reminder note a few days before the event (see samples below).

## Things To Consider

It's important to encourage families to visit as many classrooms as they'd like, not just their own children's classrooms. Provide child care for toddlers and infants, as well as refreshments in the cafeteria.

## Materials & Facilities

- Any consumable materials and supplies needed for classroom science stations
- Large-scale map indicating the science theme in each classroom; small copies to provide to families
- Refreshments (optional)

**SAMPLE 10.1** ***LETTER TO FAMILIES***

Dear Family Members and Family Friends,

Have you ever wondered about light, and how it is that we see colors? Do you ever stare up at the sky wondering how the constellations came to be? Have you ever seen the Pacific Ocean under a microscope?

Throughout our school, children have been designing experiments and activities to find some answers to questions like these. They have been working very hard on their projects, and now they are almost ready to share their results with you at our **Family Science Night**.

Please join us on (DATE) at (TIME) for this event. Bring the whole family to this hands-on discovery center—students made it just for you!

**SAMPLE 10.2** ***REMINDER TO FAMILIES AND NONTEACHING STAFF***

REMINDER!

The students at (NAME) School are eager to share their hard work and science demonstrations with you. Don't miss **Family Science Night** on (DATE) at (TIME). That's next (DAY) . . . we'll see you there!

ACTIVITY 11

# Family Math

Family Math is a widely used parent involvement program developed by EQUALS at the Lawrence Hall of Science of the University of California at Berkeley. Together, parents and children attend a series of hands-on workshops where they use math manipulatives such as blocks, beans, pennies, and other easy-to-find objects to understand more about numbers and space and to develop strategies for solving mathematics problems.

---

## Why This Activity?

Family Math is a way for parents and children to enjoy discovering math together and, in doing so, to learn to solve problems, experiment with new ideas, and help each other. For parents, the workshops offer a relaxed environment where they can enjoy learning with their children and can gather activity ideas that the family can explore at home. Students benefit from a stronger connection between what goes on in school and at home, and are likely to find more enjoyment in learning math.

## The Program

### *Getting Ready*

If your school decides to conduct a Family Math program, we strongly recommend the publication *Family Math*, available from the Lawrence Hall of Science at the University of California at Berkeley (see Outside Resources below). This resource book for teachers and parents offers almost 300 pages of specific Family Math activities. Have the book available when you introduce the Family Math idea to the teaching staff.

### *Inviting Parents*

While the Family Math program recommends that schools sponsor six to eight family sessions throughout the year, we encourage you to experiment with a smaller number—even one or two workshops—if your time is limited. When inviting parents to a Family Math program, recognize that many may be anxious about their own math skills. Be sure to invite parents in a reassuring and inclusive manner that highlights this activity as a way to have fun, enjoy spending time as a family, and learn together—not one where people have to demonstrate their math skills!

### *Planning Math Activities*

The *Family Math* book activities can be used at the workshops or described on handouts for home activities. If teachers are using hands-on, discovery-based approaches to teaching math, select Family Math activities that reinforce what students are already learning in class. Consider organizing the workshops around specific mathematical themes, such as counting, odd and even numbers, fractions, measuring, and so on. We recommend dividing participants into three different grade-level groups (for example, K–1, 2–3, 4–5) and providing for families with limited English proficiency.

### *The Workshop*

Welcome families as they come in, and provide them with a colored ticket indicating which room they should go to for their Family Math activities (this gives you an opportunity to direct students of different grade levels to an age-appropriate topic, or to offer families with limited English proficiency the opportunity to work in a bilingual room). At the first Family Math event, spend a few minutes talking about the goals and value of the program, and offer a warm-up activity to help parents and children feel comfortable. The rest of the workshop time can then be spent on the specific math activities, but consider saving some time at the end of the evening for discussing ways that parents might incorporate more math at home with their children (see below).

### *Family Reflections*

Leave time at the end of your Family Math evenings for families to talk about what they liked, what they learned, and how it felt to work together. When parents spend a few minutes reflecting on their experience, they are more likely to see its value and to enjoy sharing their excitement with others.

### *Helping Parents Follow Up at Home*

Encourage parents to provide a special place for study, to be ready to talk with their children about mathematics, to be more concerned with the process of doing mathematics than with getting the right answer, to keep their comments positive and encouraging, and to model a positive attitude about math. Also remind parents of the many day-to-day ways they can "do" math with their children—counting things as they walk around the neighborhood, measuring ingredients, dividing dessert, and so on.

## Adaptations

The Family Math approach can be easily adapted to other subjects such as science, where families explore hands-on science activities together, or art, where families learn new ideas for creative projects they can work on together. For additional ideas, see Activity 9: Family Read-Aloud, Activity 10: Family Science Night, and Activity 5: Family Projects Fair.

## Parent Information

Plan to send home an initial workshop announcement that explains the goals of Family Math, a follow-up reminder about a week before the workshop, and periodic home activities and messages of encouragement (see samples below).

## Materials & Facilities

- Math materials such as manipulatives, graph paper, rulers, measuring units
- Easy-to-find materials such as beads, blocks, pennies, toothpicks, beans
- Handouts describing activity ideas that parents and children can work on at home

## Outside Resources

*Family Math* is available from the Lawrence Hall of Science at the University of California at Berkeley. For more information, call 510-642-1823.

**SAMPLE 11.1** ***LETTER TO FAMILIES***

Dear Family Members and Family Friends,

On (DATE) we will be hosting our first schoolwide **Family Math** workshop. Family Math is a whole collection of game-like math activities that show parents and children how to explore math together. Whether you loved or hated math as a student, and no matter what you think of your math skills, we think you'll really enjoy doing these activities with your children.

Schools that offer Family Math workshops have found that children are enjoying math and spending more time on their homework. But above all, Family Math is designed to be a time to enjoy thinking and learning together as a family.

Please plan to come for an evening that is both meaningful and fun. We'll see you at (TIME) on (DATE) in the school cafeteria.

**SAMPLE 11.2 *REMINDER***

REMINDER!

Come to **Family Math**—a fun evening of math games and activities for the whole family. Don't give a second thought to your math skills; Family Math is designed for everyone to enjoy.

Family Math will be held at (TIME) on (DATE). We hope to see you there!

ACTIVITY 12

# Family Film Night

Family Film Night brings together students, their families, and school staff members for an evening of entertainment and discussion of important issues and values. Together, parents and children view one or two short films and participate in a cooperative family activity focusing on the themes and values presented in the films.

---

## Why This Activity?

By providing a forum for parents and children to enjoy a film, talk, and reflect about important values, Family Film Night fosters positive communication between parents and children. Family Film Night also helps bridge the gap that often exists between what goes on at school and what happens at home, as parents and children practice some of the learning activities that are being introduced in the classrooms—small-group discussions, cooperative learning activities, and making personal connections to values and issues highlighted in literature and film.

## The Program

### *Getting Ready*

Family Film Night is typically organized around the viewing of short films that emphasize important social values such as fairness, caring, taking responsibility, and helping others. Such films can be acquired through the school-district media center, local public library, public television station, or county office of education. Parents may also have access to appropriate films. You will have to preview any film being considered—both for its entertainment value and to make sure it will lend itself well to thoughtful discussion—and also so that you can design appropriate follow-up activities.

In many schools, Family Film Night is scheduled several times each year so that families who enjoy the activity can participate frequently.

### *Family Film Night*

Greet families as they arrive, and have them sit together either on chairs or on blankets and pillows they bring from home. Once families are seated, have the principal or an adult volunteer welcome everyone, introduce the film, and briefly describe the activities that will follow the film viewing. After the film, invite the families to participate in an activity that focuses on the important social themes raised in the film—for example, they might be given a few open-ended questions to get a family discussion going, or they might work on a cooperative project together, such as designing a collage, writing a song, or creating a skit about a central theme in the film.

If there are non-English-speaking parents in your school community, consider having a translator or providing a written translation that summarizes the film.

### *Family Reflection*

Invite participants to talk about their experience working together as a family. Ask open-ended questions, such as: What was it like to talk about the film together? What did you learn? What did you like? If the group is large or if there are several different languages being spoken, ask families to create small groups and share their experiences with others sitting near them.

## Adaptations

If the film to be shown has a corresponding book, encourage teachers to read it in class before Family Film Night; similarly, they could read other literature that addresses some of the same themes and issues raised in the film.

## Parent Information

Send home a flyer that emphasizes this event as time to enjoy as a family. A week before the Family Film Night, send a reminder that also repeats the message that this is a family event, and that children are not to be dropped off unattended (see samples below). At the event, consider giving parents a list of suggested videotapes for viewing and discussing at home as a family. If available, provide information about any films for children shown at local public libraries.

## Materials & Facilities

- Films or videos, projector or VCR, screen or large monitor
- Family activity directions, art supplies, or other materials needed
- A large, comfortable room
- Popcorn (optional)

## Outside Resources

Consider a variety of sources for relevant films, including your local public television station, public library and school-district media center. The following films have been recommended by schools that have experience organizing Family Film Nights (many of these are based on children's literature):

- *Evan's Corner*
- *The Incredible Journey*
- *Molly's Pilgrim*
- *Sarah, Plain and Tall*
- *The Sneetches*
- *Tuck Everlasting*

**SAMPLE 12.1** ***FLYER FOR FAMILIES***

Do you feel like taking your family to a Good Movie?

**Join us for Family Film Night!**

. . . where families enjoy an evening of film and activities together.

FEATURING (NAME OF FILM OR FILMS)

Family Film Night will be held on (DATE) at (TIME) in the (ROOM).

Please Note: Do not drop children off unattended. This event is for families.

**SAMPLE 12.2** ***REMINDER***

**You and your family ought to be at the pictures!**

JOIN US FOR FAMILY FILM NIGHT, FEATURING (NAME OF FILM OR FILMS)

(DATE)

(TIME)

(ROOM)

Please do not drop children off unattended.

# Taking Pride in Our Surroundings

**ACTIVITY 13** LITTER CRITTERS

**ACTIVITY 14** SCHOOLWIDE MURAL

**ACTIVITY 15** SCHOOL COMMUNITY GARDEN

There are many ways to help children learn the importance of taking responsibility in their lives. One way is to give children opportunities to practice and experience being responsible people themselves—in this case, people who care about and take responsibility for their school environment. Such activities not only show children their power to affect their environment, but also increase their commitment to school as a place where they have invested personal energy.

ACTIVITY 13

# Litter Critters

■ ***See also, Suggestions for Teachers, page 106***

Classes, entire grades, and smaller teams of students take on a variety of jobs to clean or otherwise improve the appearance of the school. Inviting every student to be on a "litter critter" team allows everyone to contribute to a positive school climate and to remember to be part of the solution, not part of the problem.

## Why This Activity?

As an ongoing schoolwide activity, Litter Critters offers students the opportunity to take responsibility for maintaining their school as a clean, pleasant place to be. By working together, children are able to see the results of their effort and feel proud that they are contributing to a cleaner school environment. The activity can also be a nice way to integrate children of all different ages and grade levels.

## The Program

The "clean-up" needs of your school will determine the specific tasks for your Litter Critters—for example, students might clean up certain areas of the school at specific times (such as at the end of the lunch hour or directly after school), or decorate the walls with posters about caring for their environment.

### *Getting Ready*

Meet with teachers and any relevant nonteaching staff, such as custodians, cafeteria workers, or playground monitors, to let them know about your plans for Litter Critters and to invite their ideas and suggestions. Brainstorm a list of possible clean-up activities, reminding teachers that activities need not be appropriate for an entire class of students. For example, some activities might be divided up among smaller classroom or cross-age Litter Critter teams, or students could participate for a week at a time before passing the job on to a new group. Distribute the suggestions for teachers and invite any feedback; invite teachers to solicit students' ideas for clean-up activities and to submit these ideas to the Litter Critter planning committee.

***Planning the Activities***

Establish a small planning committee to review the students' suggestions and make decisions about which activities are feasible and likely to be sustainable. Have the committee create a master calendar of activities, indicating which class or group will be responsible for which clean-up activity. As they plan the calendar, the committee should meet with the appropriate staff members (for example, custodians and lunchroom staff) to encourage their ideas and to coordinate details.

## Adaptations

Rather than have every class participate in the program, you might want to create one cross-grade Litter Critter team which can operate like a schoolwide club. Another possibility is to have buddy classes work together on a variety of clean-up projects.

Consider creating a Litter Critter program that goes out into the community to assist with clean-up and beautification projects, such as building a garden for a nursing home, cleaning the beach, or painting over graffiti in the school neighborhood.

## Parent Information

Let parents know about Litter Critters, and encourage them to offer their children opportunities to clean and improve their surroundings at home. Also invite their ideas for school beautification projects that families could take on together.

## Materials & Facilities

- Garbage bags, plastic gloves, recycling containers, and miscellaneous items
- Reflective vests or handmade sashes to identify Litter Critters (optional)

ACTIVITY 14

# Schoolwide Mural

■ *See also, Suggestions for Teachers, page 108*

The entire school is involved in designing and creating a wall mural to decorate the building. This project is a challenge, but it is also likely to be a great source of enjoyment and pride for students as they work together and then see their creation in the school for years to come. The mural can be redesigned every three to five years as upper-grade students move on to middle school and new students enter the school.

## Why This Activity?

Creating a mural offers students a schoolwide cooperative learning experience in which they work together on all stages of production—thinking about what they want to communicate, designing the mural, drawing up a work plan, carrying it out, and completing the project. Students are likely to experience a strong sense of pride as they see the results of their individual and cooperative efforts on the school walls each time they pass by.

## The Program

The details and logistics of creating a school mural will vary considerably from school to school. What's important is that students feel included in planning the mural, that everyone in the school community has a chance to contribute to it, and that it can be appreciated and enjoyed by the whole school.

### *Getting Ready*

At a staff meeting, propose the mural project and make sure teachers support the idea. Distribute copies of the suggestions for teachers, briefly discuss the classroom component of the activity, and invite teachers' comments and ideas. Be sure to involve the custodial staff early in the planning.

Invite a team of student and adult volunteers to do the initial planning for the creation of the mural, beginning with finding an appropriate location. Some schools have created murals on stretched canvas or portable wooden surfaces, while others have collaborated with the custodial staff to create a mural directly on hallway or courtyard walls.

The planning team could also be responsible for getting necessary materials and supplies, setting a timeline for the project, and establishing a process for choosing the mural theme. For the latter, some schools collect nominations from classrooms, while others have the planning team provide suggestions for classes to choose from. Themes should be broad enough to involve everyone and timeless enough to stay up for several years. The following, for example, focus on the school community itself: A Caring Community of Learners; Our School, Our Community; Learning Together; Ways We Care.

### *Designing the Mural*

For logistical reasons, most schools have individual classes design and paint their own sections of the mural. Once the schoolwide theme has been selected, each class submits a relevant design to the planning team, which then assigns areas of the mural space to each class.

### *Sketching the Mural*

Each section of the mural should be sketched on enlarged graph paper (or on a grid that has been drawn on large butcher paper), after which students can color in their sketch with crayons or pastels. This drawing serves as the model for the actual mural. A proportionate grid is then penciled onto the wall or mural background, so that students can re-create their design based directly on the model they have drawn on paper, one square at a time. This way the mural will be proportionate to the students' original drawing (although students can always make impromptu revisions and additions to the full-size reproduction).

### *Time To Paint*

The simplest way to organize the mural painting is to schedule time for each class to paint its section, either in rotating groups or during art classes. A master schedule will help ensure that the process runs smoothly and that each class knows its responsibilities. Schools that have done this schoolwide activity recommend having the art teacher and/or parent volunteers supervise the entire process and work with each class as needed.

### *Schoolwide Celebration*

Once the mural is complete, have a schoolwide dedication ceremony. Invite students, parents, staff, members of the community, and even the media. Include some music, refreshments, and perhaps a ribbon-cutting ceremony. Celebrate all the hard work and collaboration in your school community—and the beautiful addition to the building!

## Adaptations

Create a paper or fabric Community Quilt to which every student, classroom, or family contributes a patch designed around the theme of a caring community. (This will require that a parent, teacher, or other volunteer take responsibility for assembling the quilt with students.)

Sponsor a Sidewalk Art Festival where the entire school uses sidewalk chalk to create colorful murals on the pavement and walkways surrounding the school and playground.

## Parent Information

Inform parents of the project, and encourage them to volunteer and help the children design, paint, or display the mural. Others might be able to help solicit donations of art supplies and construction materials (see Sample 14.1 below).

## Materials & Facilities

- Art supplies, including paints, brushes, pencils, crayons or pastels, graph paper or butcher paper, containers, and smocks or old shirts
- Canvas and other structural materials, if creating a "portable" mural rather than a wall mural
- Space for creating the mural

## Outside Resources

We encourage you to take full advantage of any available resources, whether they be donated supplies or the involvement of parent volunteers, local artists, or a community agency that works in the arts. Some areas have community-based arts organizations that provide direct assistance to schools working on murals. Also consider seeking donations from local businesses and parents (particularly for smocks and containers).

## SAMPLE 14.1 *LETTER TO FAMILIES*

Dear Family Members and Family Friends,

Do you love to paint? Do you have an old smock and a paintbrush?

The students at (name) School are about to begin an ambitious project for the entire school community. It's a **Schoolwide Mural**, and they will be planning, designing, and creating it themselves. The theme for the mural is "(THEME)," and it will decorate the wall along the (PART OF THE BUILDING).

But we need your help! We're looking for parents, friends, and community members who want to get involved and make this mural a success. Please complete the attached form and return it to school as soon as possible. Thanks!

PLEASE RETURN TO YOUR CHILD'S TEACHER

Name: ______________________________

Name of Child: ______________________________

Phone: (h)______________________ (w)______________________

We need your help to create the "(theme)" mural! Please check each item below that you are interested in helping with.

- ☐ Donating a smock, old shirt(s), paintbrushes, or containers
- ☐ Building the structure for the mural on (date)
- ☐ Helping the class design and paint their section (date to be announced)
- ☐ Soliciting donations from art supply stores and businesses
- ☐ Contacting a local artist who might be interested in getting involved
- ☐ Sorry! I am unable to assist with this particular project. Please keep me informed about ways to be involved in the future.

ACTIVITY 15

# School Community Garden

■ *See also, Suggestions for Teachers, page 110*

A school community garden can be as big as a truck farm or as small as a set of window boxes. Whatever its scale, a school garden or landscaping project involves the entire school in creating a beautiful addition to the school. This highly visible tribute to the school community's pride in itself and its environment is exciting to initiate and satisfying to maintain.

## Why This Activity?

The sense of shared purpose in starting and maintaining a school garden or landscaping project can be a powerful way to build community feeling—and as the garden flourishes, the gift of everyone's individual and cooperative efforts will be obvious. By working together, students, parents, and staff members really can make their school a beautiful place. And if teachers are interested, creating a school garden lends itself to a number of possibilities for integrating curriculum.

## The Program

No matter what the ambitions for a School Community Garden, the investigating and planning stages are crucial to the project's eventual success—both for building widespread commitment to the project and for designing a feasible plan. Students should have a central role in these early stages of the project, since their ongoing commitment to the garden will determine its success. Throughout the year, classrooms can rotate weekly maintenance of the garden, and teachers at every grade level can connect various learning activities to the garden.

### *Getting Ready*

Let teachers know about your plans to create a school garden, and invite their suggestions and feedback. Ask teachers to discuss ideas for the garden with their students and to submit students' ideas to the planning committee. Distribute copies of the suggestions for teachers to stimulate discussion about ways the classroom curriculum could be tied into the garden project and how student interest and commitment can be encouraged and sustained. Establish a timeline for planning the garden. Invite nonteaching staff members as well as families to planting day (see Sample 15.2 below).

### *Planning the Garden*

A team of students, parents, staff members, and other volunteers with a particular interest in gardening should form a planning team that reviews the suggestions submitted by the classrooms. Their challenge will be to incorporate ideas from all the classrooms into a master plan for the school. The master plan should create a truly community-wide effort—that is, not a patchwork of side-by-side classroom plots or designated areas of classroom-by-classroom responsibilities. (The only exception might be in cases where window boxes are the most desirable way for the school to undertake a gardening project.)

An important part of the planning process will be budgetary. Team members will want to augment any budget as much as possible through donations or discounts from local gardening and supply businesses, by arranging for the free use of specialized equipment, and through donations of expertise and labor.

The planning team's eventual master plan should be reviewed by the school administrator and head custodian. Then a planting date should be set and a schedule established for students to care for the garden throughout the year. For example, classes could rotate weeks or areas of responsibility for the garden, or students could participate in an after-school club that works on this and other school beautification projects.

### *Planting Day*

Plan this activity for a Saturday and expect it to take the full day (not that everyone will be there all the time). Parent volunteers could act as team leaders for preparing different areas of the garden or for accomplishing particular tasks, such as constructing raised beds or rototilling the entire garden. Again, however, it's important that everyone feel connected to the garden project as a whole, not just to a specific part of it.

### *Ribbon-Cutting Ceremony*

Once the garden is planted, why not celebrate with a dedication or ribbon-cutting ceremony? Have the principal or another speaker recognize the hard work and good will that have gone into the beginning of a new source of pride for the school community.

## Adaptations

Consider a Bulb-Planting Day if your school is unable to plant a community garden. Or, if your school does not have the resources or space to create a garden, explore the possibility of volunteering as a school community to assist the Department of Parks and Recreation, a nursing home, a community center, or any other agency with an existing garden or renovation project.

Another possible beautification project is Paint-a-School, a weekend event when the entire school community is invited to paint the classrooms and hallways of their school. On Monday morning, everyone returns to clean, bright, newly painted classrooms. This kind of event requires careful planning with the district's building operations team, as well as the custodial staff at school.

## Parent Information

Many parents will enjoy participating in this project, especially if they have experience with gardening, landscaping, or building. In a letter to parents, encourage them to contribute their skills and enthusiasm. Ask parents to become involved in planting, soliciting donated tools and plants, or preparing refreshments on the day of the event. Encourage their participation again in a follow-up notification of the planting day (see samples below). Also consider ways to help make parents feel welcomed and appreciated for their participation.

## Things to Consider

Since food is always an effective community builder, you might want to combine the day with a picnic lunch. Ask parents to bring their family's lunch, and have the school provide drinks or snacks.

## Materials & Facilities

- Tools, hoses, and other supplies or equipment borrowed from parents or donated by local businesses
- Soil, compost, fertilizer, seeds, plants, and so forth

## Outside Resources

Whether your school is rural or urban, explore the possibility of having a corporate or small-business sponsor, or develop a partnership with a local garden-supply store. Some schools have received assistance from professional garden and landscape associations.

### SAMPLE 15.1 LETTER TO FAMILIES AND STAFF

Dear Family Members and Friends,

Our school community is about to begin a very exciting project, and we'd like to invite you to become involved.

In (MONTH), we will design and plant (NAME) School's first **School Community Garden** for everyone to take care of and enjoy. We are looking forward to digging in the dirt and making our garden flourish!

The garden will take a lot of planning and coordination, so we are asking students, parents, and staff members to volunteer to join the planning team. This team will incorporate ideas from all of the classrooms into a master garden plan for the school, help raise funds and donations from the community, and coordinate "Planting Day," tentatively scheduled for Saturday, (DATE).

If you are interested in getting involved, please join us for a planning meeting on (DATE) at (TIME) in the school library. Or, call (COORDINATOR) at (PHONE), if you are unable to make it to the meeting but would like to help. Please feel free to bring a friend or neighbor who might like to join us!

**SAMPLE 15.2** ***LETTER TO FAMILIES AND STAFF***

**JOIN US!**

(NAME) School is planting a

# School Community Garden

. . . and everyone's invited to join in the fun!

DATE: (DATE)
TIME: (TIME)

**PLEASE BRING:**
garden tools (label all items) • picnic lunch for your family • clothes to get messy

**WE'LL PROVIDE:**
garden tools • seeds and plants • lemonade

Bring your whole family!

* rain date is (DATE)

# 4 Suggestions for Teachers

These resource pages offer teachers practical suggestions for introducing schoolwide activities to their students and executing the classroom components of the projects. We hope these suggestions help teachers in their efforts to link classroom learning to the goals of schoolwide community-building activities and to provide students with meaningful opportunities to think, learn, and reflect, both as a community and as individuals.

# In This Chapter


| | |
|---|---|
| ACTIVITY 1 | PEOPLE WHO MAKE IT WORK |
| ACTIVITY 2 | WELCOMING NEWCOMERS |
| ACTIVITY 3 | BUDDIES PROGRAM |
| ACTIVITY 4 | FAMILY HERITAGE MUSEUM |
| ACTIVITY 5 | FAMILY PROJECTS FAIR |
| ACTIVITY 6 | GRANDPERSONS GATHERING |
| ACTIVITY 7 | ADOPT-A-FAMILY |
| ACTIVITY 8 | WORKING FOR A CAUSE |
| ACTIVITY 10 | FAMILY SCIENCE NIGHT |
| ACTIVITY 13 | LITTER CRITTERS |
| ACTIVITY 14 | SCHOOLWIDE MURAL |
| ACTIVITY 15 | SCHOOL COMMUNITY GARDEN |

ACTIVITY 1 SUGGESTIONS FOR TEACHERS

# People Who Make it Work

In each classroom students interview their teacher and one or more of the nonteaching school staff members and then create vivid displays for a whole-school collage that captures the voices and faces of every adult in the school community. The goal of this activity is to help students get to know the adults they see at school every day—teachers, secretaries, administrators, nurses, librarians, playground monitors, lunchroom staff, classroom aides, social workers, bus drivers, and the custodial staff. The displays can include photographs, drawings, stories, poems, or whatever else fits the interests and ambitions of the collage makers.

---

*Below are some suggestions for doing the classroom component of this schoolwide activity. Please feel free to adapt or change them to fit the needs of your students.*

## Introducing the Activity

Have students brainstorm a list of the various adult members of their school community. What do the adults do in the school? What do the students know about these adults?

Describe the schoolwide project to students, and ask them to think about the idea of interviewing these members of the school community. Make sure that students understand how this schoolwide project will work, and encourage their questions and ideas.

## Preparing for the Interviews

Tell students that they will begin by interviewing you, and then they will interview another staff person. Ask students to think about what they would like to know about their interview subjects, what they would like to include in their displays to introduce these people to the rest of the school, and what kinds of questions they need to ask to get this information. (Explain that they will have about 20 minutes for each interview.) Have students brainstorm these ideas, and list the categories of information they would like to address. Then have the students list the questions they will ask in each category.

Encourage students to think about the process of interviewing the adults and documenting the information. How would they like to conduct the interview? How can everybody in the class participate, either by asking questions, recording responses, creating the collage piece, and so on? How would they like to record the information from the interviews? For example, the class may want to have a camera on hand to take pictures, a tape recorder to tape the interview, or even a video camera. They may want to take turns taking notes during the interview, or take notes afterwards as a class, to help remember what was said.

Before the interview, have a brief conversation with any visiting staff people to let them know about the questions students have decided to ask—especially if the questions will be personal, such as what their family likes to do together, or what they like most about being at school. Also tell them if they will be asked to lend photographs or other artifacts for the display.

## Follow-Up

After the interview, invite students to discuss the experience. What went well? What did they learn? What did they enjoy most? Collect student responses on chart paper, or have a student recorder do so, in case you want to share your experience with another class or the rest of the school.

## Creating the Collage Pieces

Have students work together in pairs or small groups to prepare a display about the adults they interviewed. Encourage drawing, magazine cuttings, poetry, writing, favorite quotes, illustrations, painting, photographs, or any other ideas students contribute. Let students know beforehand what the final size of each class display is to be, so that everyone's contribution is likely to fit in.

## Sharing Our Work with Others

Once the displays are finished, and before they are integrated into the school collage, consider partnering with another classroom to give students the opportunity to present their displays and talk about how they interviewed the adults and created the representations. This "extra step" enables students to feel proud of their work, to teach each other, and to learn more about some adults who will be featured in the larger school collage.

**ACTIVITY 2** **SUGGESTIONS FOR TEACHERS**

# Welcoming Newcomers

This activity helps new students, especially those who arrive midyear, to feel a part of their new school community. A group of students representing their respective classrooms—the "Welcomers Committee"—creates the plan for introducing new students to their school, whether through a partner program, a school tour, a school community information packet, or a combination of ideas. When left to design and be responsible for their own ways to welcome new students, children react generously, calling on their own understanding of the difficulties of entering a new situation.

---

*Below are some suggestions for preparing your class to participate in this schoolwide activity. Please feel free to adapt or change them to fit the needs of your students.*

## Introducing the Activity

Once your students have had the chance to begin to get to know each other (but still early in the school year), have a class discussion about how it feels to be a new student. You might ask them to remember back to how they felt at the beginning of the school year. Then ask them to imagine what it would be like to enter a new school after the school year has started. In what ways might it feel similar? In what ways might it feel different?

Ask students to think about and discuss what would make them feel more comfortable if they were entering a new school midyear. What might an entire class do to help them feel welcome? What might individual students do? Then have students talk about what kinds of things they would do to help a new student feel welcome and included.

For a writing project, you could propose the themes: "A time when someone made me feel welcome or included" or "A time when I helped someone feel welcome or included." You can gather and bind students' contributions to make a class book on the subject.

Read a story or poem about what it feels like to be a newcomer, and then discuss the reading with the class. The following are some picture and read-aloud books that highlight this issue:

***Picture Books***

- *One Frog Too Many*, by Mercer and Marianna Mayer
- *Ruby the Copycat*, by Peggy Rathmann
- *Say Hello, Vanessa*, by Marjorie Weinman Sharmat

***Grades 3–5***

- *The Hundred Dresses*, by Eleanor Estes
- *In the Year of the Boar and Jackie Robinson*, by Bette Bao Lord
- *Crow Boy*, by Taro Yashima

## Nominating Welcomers

Explain that while only a few students will be taking part in the official Welcomers Committee, all students can take initiative to help newcomers feel welcome. If your school has decided to let students choose representatives from their classrooms to be on the Welcomers Committee, help students decide as a class on a fair process for choosing.

## Ongoing Activities

You may want to give the representatives to the Welcomers Committee the opportunity to ask the class for feedback and suggestions about welcoming newcomers; you might also have them regularly report back to the class about the activities and progress of the committee.

Ask the representatives to the committee to keep the class informed about new students so that the class can prepare a special welcome for that person, such as a card, poster, or a visit to say hello.

ACTIVITY 3 SUGGESTIONS FOR TEACHERS

# Buddies Program

Every student in the school is matched with an older or younger "buddy" for a variety of activities that allow the two children to develop a special kind of friendship—one that is outside of the usual classroom, family, and neighborhood circles. Activities are chosen for their academic and social value and are carefully planned to ensure that buddies get to know one another, build trust, and feel comfortable learning together.

---

*Below are some suggestions for preparing your class to participate in this schoolwide activity. Please feel free to adapt or change them to fit the needs of your students.*

## Getting Started

### *Pairing Students*

Work with the teacher of your buddy class to pair the buddies; students should not be asked to choose their own buddies, as hurt feelings and other problems are likely to arise.

### *Preparing Students*

Before starting buddy activities, and before each activity, help your students understand their role and some of the difficulties they may face. For example, have students generate respectful ways to work with a buddy who is shy and doesn't want to talk, or ways to work with a buddy who spends a lot of time fooling around. After every activity, talk with students about what went well and what they could improve.

### *Choosing Activities*

Be sure to design activities that allow meaningful participation by both buddies and from which both buddies can benefit socially and academically.

## Buddy Activities

Besides the suggestions below, we also encourage you to create and co-plan your own activities with your buddy teacher and to start with as few or as many as you feel comfortable with; don't try to do them all in one year.

### *Getting-to-Know-You Activities*

Plan activities that help buddies get to know each other, such as the following:

- **Draw Your Buddy.** Provide a topic, such as "How does your buddy help at home?" or "What does your buddy like to do after school?" Have buddies interview each other about the topic, and then have them draw a picture about what they have learned.
- **Special Stories.** Ask each student to bring in a possession, memento, or any object that has personal significance, and then have buddies draw or write about each other's objects. (You might want to model this activity with your buddy teacher before asking students to bring in objects.)

### *Ongoing Activities*

Certain activities and practices can be continued throughout the school year in order to help buddies develop and strengthen their relationships.

- **Journals.** Have students keep individual buddy journals, using drawings or narrative to record their buddy experiences.
- **Bulletin Board.** Create classroom Buddy Bulletin Boards that display photographs of each pair, and add projects from each buddy activity throughout the year.
- **Pen Pals.** Establish a special mailbox for "buddy correspondence," and provide time for buddies to write letters to each other after each buddy activity. Buddies can use the mailbox at other times as well.
- **Special Times.** Have buddies attend school assemblies or events together, make special visits to the library, go to monthly buddy lunches in the cafeteria, or spend time as playground companions.
- **Academic Activities.** Many regular academic activities invite peer teaching, tutoring, and cooperative products; others can be structured as presentations for buddies or a buddy class.

### *End-of-the-Year Activities*

Make time at the end of the year for buddies to reflect together on the things they have done and to thank each other.

- **Reviewing the Year.** Give buddies time to look at things they have made together and to recall shared experiences. Ask each pair to choose a favorite activity to write about and illustrate. These products can then be compiled into a group book or mural shared by both classes.
- **Expressing Appreciation.** Each class may want to show their appreciation for their buddy class through writing or drawing, or by making a project for their buddy class. (Such gestures can be made throughout the year as well.)

## Special Considerations

### *Absences*

You can prepare for disruptions in buddy match-ups by grouping two buddy pairs into a team. Let the teams spend time together occasionally so that if someone is absent, the team will be comfortable including the student without a buddy.

### *Complaints*

You may find some students making such statements as "I don't like my buddy," "This is dumb," or "Can I switch buddies?" Although these put-down statements can be frustrating, they also represent an opportunity to teach; individual or group discussions can help get at underlying feelings and can generate suggestions for appropriate ways to express those feelings and to improve buddy interactions.

**ACTIVITY 4** **SUGGESTIONS FOR TEACHERS**

# Family Heritage Museum

Students and staff members contribute to a schoolwide display of information and artifacts that tell something about their own family heritage. At home, children and parents decide on their family's contribution to the museum by talking, telling stories, looking at photographs, and investigating their family's history together. This activity can also be a culminating event for individual classroom studies of family history and cultural heritage.

---

*Below are some suggestions for preparing your class to participate in this schoolwide activity. Please feel free to adapt or change them to fit the needs of your students.*

## Introducing the Activity

During the month before the Family Heritage Museum opens, encourage students to talk with their parents or other significant adults about their family history, traditions, knowledge, and life experiences. Consider using the questions below, perhaps asking students to discuss one of these topics at a time (one each week), so that families can focus their stories and have enough time for these discussions. As students begin to take these questions home to discuss, you might also want to spend some time in class role-playing a child and parent having a discussion about their family background. Please feel free to add your own or your students' ideas to these suggested questions for discussion:

- What was it like to be my age? What were some of your favorite things to do? How are things different now?
- Tell me a story about something that happened when you were growing up.
- What stories do you remember about people in our family? Can you tell me a funny, sad, or surprising story about one of our relatives?
- What are some important things that you learned from your parents (my grandparents), or from other relatives? What are some important things that you've learned in your own life from experience?

## Invitations to Families

The Coordinating Team will prepare an announcement and follow-up reminders for teachers to send home, to describe the project and invite families to create a display and visit the museum. In class, make sure students understand that they are not restricted to using artifacts for their displays; they can choose from many alternatives to show their family heritage, such as creating a drawing, poster, or story about their family. This is particularly important for recent immigrants and children who are not living with parents, as they might not have access to objects that represent their family traditions and heritage.

## Supporting Activities

In class, students could tell their family stories to partners, small groups, or the whole class. You could also have children write or draw pictures about what they've learned, and then compile this work into a class book about family heritage. (If you do make a class book, send a copy home with each child.) The book or individual student work could be displayed at the Family Heritage Museum.

Several days before the museum opening, give students a chance to talk about their family's display with a partner. This can be a useful way of discovering any problems that a child is having in trying to create a display.

Consider partnering with another class to give children an opportunity to present some of their work before the museum event. Your students could read from their stories, read from the class book, show pictures, and answer questions.

**ACTIVITY 5** SUGGESTIONS FOR TEACHERS

# Family Projects Fair

A Family Projects Fair begins with families deciding on a cooperative project to do at home—for example, they might document a project that they work on together, such as planting a garden; create a project such as a science experiment or model; or make a display about a family interest, such as baseball or rock collecting. The emphasis should be on the process of working together as a family, rather than on the resulting "product." Families then show their projects at school for the Family Projects Fair, during which they can both explain their work to other families in the school community and learn from the other families' projects.

---

*Below are some suggestions for preparing your class to participate in this schoolwide activity. Please feel free to adapt or change them to fit the needs of your students.*

## Introducing the Activity

Tell the students about the Family Projects Fair and how it will work. Then ask students to describe projects—big and small—they have worked on with their families in the past. Ask students what they accomplished, made, or investigated together, and how they liked working as a family. Open up the discussion to include projects that students might have worked on cooperatively with siblings, friends, grandparents, or any other important people.

Have students brainstorm ideas for projects they might create at home with their families. You could get them started by reading project ideas from the letter to be sent home or by suggesting project categories. Record ideas for all to see, and encourage students to add them to the list of suggestions on their letter home. Remind students not to decide on a project during class—that families are to decide together and that more than one family can work on the same idea.

## Supporting an Emphasis on Cooperation

Model the planning process with students by selecting one idea as a class and planning how to execute it. Ask the class, for example: If your family decided to do this project, how would you begin? What would be some of your first steps? Consider having students role-play a family in the process of starting a project. Remind students of the importance of inviting everyone in the family to participate and to contribute ideas.

Read and discuss the enclosure that will accompany the letter to families about the fair, called "Five Suggestions for Choosing and Organizing a Cooperative Family Project" (see Sample 5.2 on page 38). Ask such questions as: How are these suggestions similar to the way we do cooperative work in our class? Can you think of any other important things to keep in mind? Have students work in small groups to practice explaining these guidelines in their own words or to illustrate them.

Establish a weekly time for students to talk about how their family projects are going, either in pairs, small groups, or as a whole class. Here are some questions you might want to ask:

- What are you enjoying most about working on this project? What are other family members enjoying the most?
- Are there any difficulties that have come up? How have they been resolved?
- What are you learning from your projects? What do you want to learn more about?

## Special Considerations

If some children's parents are too busy for or have not demonstrated interest in the project, it may help to suggest ideas for simple projects these students could initiate themselves, as well as specific ways to involve other family members such as siblings or other relatives.

Other people who could work with students on a project include nonteaching school staff, high school students, and community groups such as Big Brother/Big Sister. For children who attend before- or after-school programs, find out whether the staff of those programs could incorporate such projects into their program.

**ACTIVITY 6** SUGGESTIONS FOR TEACHERS

# Grandpersons Gathering

Grandpersons Gathering is a time for students to celebrate a special relationship they have with a grandparent or other adult "grandperson." Students invite a grandparent or an older friend, neighbor, or relative to be their guest at school for an afternoon. Various activities foster an open exchange between children and the visitor, introduce the grandpersons to the school community, and help teachers and staff members learn more about the significant adults in children's lives.

---

*Below are some suggestions for doing the classroom component of this schoolwide activity. Please feel free to adapt or change them to fit the needs of your students.*

## Introducing the Activity

To set the tone for this activity, read aloud some books that highlight relationships between children and older adults, such as the books suggested below (many of the picture books are suitable for children of all ages). Use the books as a starting point for students' discussion about their own significant relationships with grandparents or older people; for example, ask students about the similarities and differences between their own relationships and those portrayed in the stories.

### *Picture Books*

- *Song and Dance Man*, by Karen Ackerman
- *Stina's Visit*, by Lena Anderson
- *The Wednesday Surprise*, by Eve Bunting
- *Bigmama's*, by Donald Crews
- *The Patchwork Quilt*, by Valerie Flournoy
- *Niki's Little Donkey*, by Coby Hol
- *Uncle Jed's Barbershop*, by Margaree Mitchell
- *Chicken Sunday*, by Patricia Polacco
- *Miss Maggie*, by Cynthia Rylant

- *Storm in the Night*, by Mary Stolz
- *I Know a Lady*, by Charlotte Zolotow

### Grades 3–4

- *Taking Care of Yoki*, by Barbara Campbell
- *Justin and the Best Biscuits in the World*, by Mildred Pitts Walter

### Grades 5–7

- *Cousins*, by Virginia Hamilton
- "At the Home" in *Throwing Shadows*, by E.L. Konigsburg
- *To Hell with Dying*, by Alice Walker

## Planning the Event with the Class

You can include the class in planning the event by suggesting the following ideas and asking for responses and other suggestions. Encourage students to think about the visitors they might invite and what special skills, interests, or histories those people may want to share with the class.

### Interviews

Working in pairs or small groups, students could interview grandpersons about their lives, their families, their childhoods, and what they enjoy doing.

Before the gathering, the whole class could brainstorm ideas about what to ask in the interviews, and then after the interviews children could introduce their grandpersons to the rest of the class. If students have access to a video camera, they might videotape the interviews and edit them together. Reports, art projects, and creative writing could all follow from this activity.

Upper-grade students could approach the visits specifically as an opportunity to gather oral history. Although students can't see the past, grandpersons did—what would students like to know? As students prepare a list of questions for their visitors, have them draw upon what they already know or think they know about history and society 30 to 50 years ago. Have them consider what things have changed and what things may have stayed the same.

### Storytelling

Students could invite grandpersons to tell a story—perhaps a tale about growing up, a favorite folktale, or a published story that is fun to tell aloud.

### *Share an Artifact*

Students could ask grandpersons to bring an artifact—any object of personal significance—and to tell a story about the object. For example, a grandperson might bring something he or she has made and talk about the process of making it; another might bring an old doll, photo album, or family heirloom as the centerpiece of a family story. Students could bring in artifacts as well and, in small groups, exchange stories with grandpersons.

### *Art Project*

Students and grandpersons could work together in small groups on a simple, easily completed art project such as a mural, diorama, or handmade book. The project could be prompted by a story that is read aloud or a film that is shown to the entire class beforehand, or it could be based on the grandperson interviews described above. Grandpersons could also be invited to share a skill they have.

## Scheduling the Day

As a class you may decide to have a few different activities taking place consecutively or simultaneously in various activity centers around the room—for example, one center for interviewing, another for storytelling, another for art projects, and another for skill demonstrations.

If you decide to use activity centers, we recommend that you still provide time for whole-class discussions or activities so that everyone will have some shared experiences. Some schools may also chose to sponsor a schoolwide assembly, presentation, or picnic celebration for everyone.

## Follow-Up Activities

You may want to invite students to work in small groups to write thank-you letters to the grandpersons who visited. Each small group could be assigned to write to one or two grandpersons and to describe some of the things they most enjoyed about the grandpersons' visits to the classroom.

Visit with another class to give students the opportunity to share their Grandpersons Gathering experiences informally with others. Students may want to share stories they've written, results of interviews, artwork, or just a short account of the day's highlights.

**ACTIVITY 7** **SUGGESTIONS FOR TEACHERS**

# Adopt-a-Family

Adopt-a-Family allows the entire school community to think about and attend to the needs of others. In collaboration with a local social service agency, each classroom is matched with a family in need of such basic items as clothes, food, books, and toys. Each class then takes responsibility for deciding how to assist this family. Although schools typically initiate this program during the holiday season, classrooms often choose to continue providing support for their family throughout the year.

---

*Below are some suggestions for preparing your class to participate in this schoolwide activity. Please feel free to adapt or change them to fit the needs of your students.*

## Setting the Tone

It's very important to set the tone for this activity from the beginning: the goal of helping is to affirm our connections with each other, not to encourage feelings of superiority. You may want to begin by leading the class in a discussion about receiving and giving help, using the questions below as guidelines. Remember to share your own thoughts with your students as a way to help them feel comfortable sharing their ideas and feelings. Record and categorize these responses, with your students' help, and please feel free to add your own questions to this list of suggestions:

- How does it feel to help others? Why?
- What does it feel like to receive help from someone when you need it?
- Are there ways that people can make us feel bad, even when they're trying to help?
- How can someone help without making us feel bad about ourselves?
- When we help others, what can we remember to do so that people feel good about being helped?

## Introducing the Activity

After discussing how it feels to give and receive help, you may want to help children focus on the idea that all of us, no matter how much or how little we own, have something to offer. Explain the Adopt-a-Family effort and how the class can participate.

Ask students to think about the difference between material and nonmaterial giving. Have them brainstorm a list of material things they can give and then a list of nonmaterial ways they can help. Make a class list for each category.

Have students talk with a partner about a time when someone helped them feel better by giving them something nonmaterial—spending time with them, teaching them a new skill, reading them a story, offering their friendship, making them laugh, playing a game with them, and so on. Then invite students to share their partners' stories with the rest of the class (remind students to ask permission before sharing). Students may also want to write or draw about the special gifts they and their partner have received.

Ask students if they have anything to add to the original class list of nonmaterial gifts. Keep the list on display and add students' new ideas throughout the next few weeks.

## Helping Our "Adopted" Family

Once you have set the tone with the activities described above, help students decide as a class how they would like to help their "adopted" family. Give students all the information you have about the family members, and lead a discussion about different possibilities for helping them. These might include donating food, clothing, or toys; raising money to purchase gifts; or sending handmade items such as cards, stories, or artwork. Help the class choose an initial helping activity and perhaps other activities for later in the year.

**ACTIVITY 8** **SUGGESTIONS FOR TEACHERS**

# Working for a Cause

Each school picks a "helping" opportunity that interests its students and staff—such as collecting supplies for disaster victims, raising money for a cause, or working together on a community service project such as a toy drive or walk-a-thon. Students apply their considerable energy and ingenuity to a cause that lets them reach out and contribute to the wider community.

---

*Below are some suggestions for preparing your class to participate in this schoolwide activity. Please feel free to adapt or change them to fit the needs of your students.*

## Setting the Tone

While this activity is not as personal as Adopt-a-Family, it creates an excellent opportunity for classroom discussion about giving and receiving help and about the benefits of working together. Consider the following suggestions for a class discussion:

- Ask students to think of a time when they or their families needed help and were able to receive it. How did it feel to need help? How did it feel to receive help?
- Ask students to think of a time when they or their families were able to help someone else. How did it feel to be able to help?
- Ask students to think of a time when they participated in a group effort to help others, such as a walk-a-thon, soup kitchen, or clean-up drive. How did it feel to work on a community project with others?

## Introducing the Activity

Explain the Working for a Cause activity to your students, describing the cause the school has decided to focus on and how each class will participate. You might want to tell students about the other helping opportunities that were considered and the reasons that this one was selected.

Ask students to brainstorm ways they could participate in the helping effort. Encourage them to think of different categories of helping, such as fund-raising, collecting supplies, or sending cards (this will vary depending on the cause).

Lead a discussion about these categories and ideas, and help the students make a decision about what they would like to do together. Younger students might simply be presented with the question, "What can we do to help?"

## Raising Money (optional)

If the chosen activity requires students to raise money, then you can increase students' commitment to the fund-raising effort by inviting their own ideas about how to proceed. Have students brainstorm a list of possibilities, such as bake sales, walk-a-thons, car washes, and flea markets. Encourage them to consider attention-grabbing approaches as well, such as Mile of Quarters. (This event could be arranged in collaboration with a local mall or shopping area, where passersby add quarters to a growing line of coins until a mile-long chain of quarters is collected.)

## Reflecting on the Experience

After the project has been completed, give students the opportunity to reflect on the experience during an informal class discussion. Ask students questions such as: What did we learn from this project? What did we enjoy most about it? Were there any things we would do differently next time?

ACTIVITY 10 SUGGESTIONS FOR TEACHERS

# Family Science Night

Family Science Night is a high-involvement "messing around" time for children and their parents. Together, families make their way from classroom to classroom exploring a variety of hands-on science activities that students have created in class during the weeks leading up to the event.

---

*Below are some suggestions for doing the classroom component of this schoolwide activity. Please feel free to adapt or change them to fit the needs of your students.*

## Introducing the Activity

After the staff has set general parameters for the Family Science Night and everyone is clear about the science focus in each of the classrooms, introduce this activity to your students. Make available to the students descriptions of a wide variety of activities related to your class's science topic. Help your students choose three or four of the activities to work on. With upper-grade students, also encourage them to brainstorm their own project ideas as a class.

## Creating Science Centers

Once the activities have been selected, you may want to involve the whole class in a more in-depth discussion of each activity. Generate ideas for each activity and brainstorm a list of materials that will be needed, how these materials might be acquired, problems that might arise, and possible solutions. Then have students form groups that will be responsible for creating and setting up each science station.

Once students have done some initial planning for their activity center, they could present their ideas to the class for feedback and suggestions. This would be a good time for the class to brainstorm such questions as: What kinds of questions might visitors to the center have? What will they need to know? What might they like to know?

Encourage students to create signs and posters identifying their station, explaining background information, presenting instructions, and providing answers to common questions that were raised in the class discussion. Remind students to present posters and signs in all of the home languages that are represented in the classroom.

Students may also want to create a logbook for each center, in which visiting parents and family members can write about their experiences, their questions, what they learned, and what they enjoyed.

## Building Schoolwide Anticipation

Give students the opportunity to form small groups and visit other classrooms to give brief (five-minute) presentations about the center they are working on or have completed. This will let students know about what is happening in other classrooms and will raise their interest in attending Family Science Night. Then on the night of the event, students are likely to remember the presentations and to encourage their families to visit the other classrooms as well as their own.

## Logistics for the Event

Work with students to create a schedule for staffing their activity centers. All students will then have the opportunity to teach others and also to visit the rest of the activity centers throughout the school with their families.

## Reflection and Appreciation

Make sure to have some time after the event for students to reflect upon and appreciate what went well, talk about what they learned, and feel a sense of satisfaction about their work and cooperation. You may also want to ask students what they would do differently next time.

ACTIVITY 13 SUGGESTIONS FOR TEACHERS

# Litter Critters

Classes, entire grades, and smaller teams of students take on a variety of jobs to clean or otherwise improve the appearance of the school. Inviting every student to be on a "litter critter" team allows everyone to contribute to a positive school climate and to remember to be part of the solution, not part of the problem.

---

*Below are some suggestions for preparing your class to participate in this schoolwide activity. Please feel free to adapt or change them to fit the needs of your students.*

## Introducing the Activity

Have a discussion with your students about litter in general. How do they feel and what do they think when they see that a place has been littered? When they see a place that is clean?

Ask students to brainstorm a list of reasons why people might litter and thereby ruin their environment. Ask students for examples of where they have seen litter in their school or other instances of people not taking responsibility for their environment. What might be done to prevent this problem?

Introduce the schoolwide program to the class, and ask students to brainstorm a list of different clean-up activities they might be able to do around the school. Explain that all classes will send their ideas to the Litter Critter planning team, which will choose which activities to focus on and create a schedule so that all students can take turns at the different jobs that help keep the school clean.

## Ongoing Activities

Once the planning team has arranged a schoolwide schedule, take some time each month to review your class's responsibilities. As much as possible, let the students themselves decide how to organize their work.

After completing tasks or a cycle of a clean-up activities, give students time to review their experiences. How did their work go? What did they learn from it? Do they have any suggestions or recommendations as a result of their experience on the job? (Their suggestions could be addressed to the school as a whole, the next team that will do the job, the Litter Critter planning committee, or the school administration.)

If your school has decided to sponsor a Litter Critters club rather than involving all classes, ask club members in your class to share their experiences with their classmates. Encourage questions and discussion.

After your students have completed a task or cycle of clean-up activities, have students write a letter to, or create illustrations for, the next class or group of students that will be doing that job. Based on their experiences, what advice would they offer? What did they learn? What was the most fun? What was the most challenging? Why? What would they do differently next time?

Design academic experiences (science, math, social studies, art, and so on) around the litter collection. For example, have students classify or categorize the litter, hypothesize about the cause of the different kinds of litter, and design a campaign to decrease specific types of litter.

ACTIVITY 14 SUGGESTIONS FOR TEACHERS

# Schoolwide Mural

The entire school is involved in designing and creating a wall mural to decorate the building. This project is a challenge, but it is also likely to be a great source of enjoyment and pride for students as they work together and then see their creation in the school for years to come. The mural can be redesigned every three to five years as upper-grade students move on to middle school and new students enter the school.

---

*Below are some suggestions for doing the classroom component of this schoolwide activity. Please feel free to adapt or change them to fit the needs of your students.*

## Introducing the Activity

Begin a class discussion by asking children if they have seen any murals in their community or elsewhere. Show students pictures of murals so that everyone has a chance to see what they look like. What do they know about murals? What do they like about murals? How are murals different than other types of paintings?

Inform the class of the plans for a schoolwide mural. Depending on the planning process being used for this activity, either ask students to brainstorm possible themes for the mural, or (if the planning committee has chosen a theme) have students brainstorm ideas for their class contribution to the mural.

## Practicing with Grids

Give students the opportunity to practice using a proportionate grid to create a mural. Demonstrate how to create and use a grid, and have students try their hand at it before beginning the "real" class mural.

For example, you might have students work in small groups to do a drawing based on a theme other than the mural theme, and have them pencil in a grid over their finished drawings. Demonstrate this for the entire class, emphasizing that students create an equal amount of space between each grid line (consider the math applications that can be integrated with this project). Then have students sketch a larger grid with evenly spaced intervals on a bigger sheet of paper. Have students re-create their design on the larger piece of paper, copying their original design one square at a time.

*Note: Kindergarten and first-grade teachers might want to just do a simple demonstration of this practice activity, but as a hands-on activity this is suitable for second grade and up.*

## Designing the Class Portion of the Mural

If your students have not already done so, have them brainstorm ideas for their mural segment (relevant to the schoolwide theme that has been chosen). Have the students agree on a design and submit a sketch to the planning committee.

If possible, use the same procedure to create the class mural segment that you used to have students "practice" doing a mural—for example, having students work in small groups on different sections of the class design. Have students create their proportionate model of the design, sketching it on enlarged graph paper (or on a grid that has been drawn on large butcher paper) and coloring it in with crayons or pastels. Then the larger grid will be penciled onto a wall or mural background, and the groups of students can replicate their sections one square at a time.

## Reflection and Appreciation

After the schoolwide mural has been completed, make some time for your students to reflect on and discuss what went well, what they learned, how they worked together, and how they feel about the new schoolwide work of art.

**ACTIVITY 15** SUGGESTIONS FOR TEACHERS

# School Community Garden

A school community garden can be as big as a truck farm or as small as a set of window boxes. Whatever its scale, a school garden or landscaping project involves the entire school in creating a beautiful addition to the school. This highly visible tribute to the school community's pride in itself and its environment is exciting for students, parents, and staff members to initiate and satisfying to maintain.

---

*Below are some suggestions for preparing your class to participate in this schoolwide activity. Please feel free to adapt or change them to fit the needs of your students.*

## Introducing the Activity

Have a general discussion with your students about gardens, and ask them to talk about gardens they have seen or worked in. What do they know about gardens? What different kinds of gardens are there, and why? What do they like about gardens? What do they want to know about gardens?

Introduce the schoolwide project to students and ask them to think about what they would like to see grow in the garden. With younger students, you might want to generate a class list of ideas that you can submit to the planning committee. Upper-grade students could generate ideas and use these as a springboard for learning more about what kinds of plants can thrive in the given soil, light, and climate conditions in your area. They could then create a list of suggestions for the garden project based on their research. In either case, make sure that students understand that the planning team will be considering the ideas of all the classrooms and making the final decisions about the garden plan.

## Ongoing Activities

At the beginning of this project, have a discussion with the children about the general concept of sharing responsibility for the garden. What would happen if only one class were responsible for taking care of the garden? What might be the benefits? What might be the burdens? You may want to discuss the proverb "Many hands make light work." What are some examples of sharing responsibility in their own lives? As the project continues, revisit these ideas if student interest or commitment seems to flag.

Try to ensure that all of the students in the class have an active role in garden maintenance during your classroom's participation in the project, or throughout the course of the year.

## Curricular Connections

You may want to design specific learning experiences for your class based around the garden. For example, students could study the changes in the garden over time, observing carefully and drawing or writing about their observations.

# 5 Resources

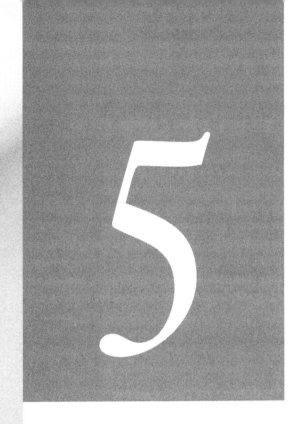

The resources that follow are designed to help your Coordinating Team create a schoolwide program that is well-organized, engaging, and fun. We encourage you to make copies of these resources and use them throughout your planning.

- Schoolwide Community-Building: A Needs Assessment Survey
- Schoolwide Activity Assessment
- Questions for the Coordinating Team
- Strategies for Increasing Parent Involvement
- Additional Schoolwide Activities

# Schoolwide Community-Building: A Needs Assessment Survey

As you know, the Coordinating Team is in the process of putting together a program of activities to build a stronger sense of community at our school. We are asking you—as an important member of the school community—to help us think about our school's strengths and weaknesses in helping children, parents, teachers, and other staff members feel at home. Please complete this survey by rating each statement (circle the number closest to your opinion). If there is any section that you are not able to complete, please feel free to leave it blank. Thank you!

---

**1** = STRONGLY DISAGREE
**2** = DISAGREE
**3** = DON'T KNOW
**4** = AGREE
**5** = STRONGLY AGREE

**STUDENTS**

| | | | | | |
|---|---|---|---|---|---|
| Most students feel a sense of belonging in classrooms and in the school | 1 | 2 | 3 | 4 | 5 |
| Most students feel cared for by other students, teachers, and adults in the school | 1 | 2 | 3 | 4 | 5 |
| Most students have the opportunity to practice "helping" behavior | 1 | 2 | 3 | 4 | 5 |
| Most students have the opportunity to interact with older and younger children | 1 | 2 | 3 | 4 | 5 |
| Most students have opportunities to take responsibility for their physical environment | 1 | 2 | 3 | 4 | 5 |
| Most students feel safe in the building and school yard | 1 | 2 | 3 | 4 | 5 |

**PARENTS/FAMILIES**

| | | | | | |
|---|---|---|---|---|---|
| Most parents/families are informed about what takes place in the classroom | 1 | 2 | 3 | 4 | 5 |
| Most parents/families have opportunities to develop trusting relationships with teachers | 1 | 2 | 3 | 4 | 5 |
| Most parents/families attend parent-teacher conferences regularly | 1 | 2 | 3 | 4 | 5 |
| Most parents/families attend activities that their children are involved in | 1 | 2 | 3 | 4 | 5 |
| Most parents/families find the school to be a welcoming place | 1 | 2 | 3 | 4 | 5 |
| Most parents/families are aware of ways positive social behavior is fostered in the school | 1 | 2 | 3 | 4 | 5 |
| Most parents/families want the school to help foster their children's growth as caring people | 1 | 2 | 3 | 4 | 5 |
| Most parents/families are aware of the importance of reading with their children at home | 1 | 2 | 3 | 4 | 5 |
| Most parents/families are concerned with their children's learning goals | 1 | 2 | 3 | 4 | 5 |
| The school provides opportunities for parents to support their children's learning | 1 | 2 | 3 | 4 | 5 |
| The school does a good job of communicating with parents | 1 | 2 | 3 | 4 | 5 |

## Schoolwide Community-Building:
A Needs Assessment Survey

### TEACHERS

| | | | | | |
|---|---|---|---|---|---|
| Most teachers involve students in helping determine the school environment | 1 | 2 | 3 | 4 | 5 |
| Most teachers encourage students to take responsibility for their learning and behavior | 1 | 2 | 3 | 4 | 5 |
| Most teachers structure ways for students to work cooperatively and help each other | 1 | 2 | 3 | 4 | 5 |
| Most teachers have positive, collaborative relationships with colleagues | 1 | 2 | 3 | 4 | 5 |
| Most teachers have the opportunity to interact with parents informally | 1 | 2 | 3 | 4 | 5 |
| Most teachers support schoolwide activities and participate freely | 1 | 2 | 3 | 4 | 5 |
| Most teachers enjoy working together to plan cross-class or schoolwide activities | 1 | 2 | 3 | 4 | 5 |
| Most teachers feel valued for their contributions | 1 | 2 | 3 | 4 | 5 |

### NONTEACHING STAFF

| | | | | | |
|---|---|---|---|---|---|
| Most staff have positive, collaborative relationships with colleagues | 1 | 2 | 3 | 4 | 5 |
| Most staff have the opportunity to interact with parents informally | 1 | 2 | 3 | 4 | 5 |
| Most staff support schoolwide activities and participate freely | 1 | 2 | 3 | 4 | 5 |
| Most staff feel valued for their contributions | 1 | 2 | 3 | 4 | 5 |
| Most staff have opportunities to get to know students as people | 1 | 2 | 3 | 4 | 5 |
| Most staff have the opportunity to understand and contribute to the school's mission | 1 | 2 | 3 | 4 | 5 |

### SCHOOL COMMUNITY

| | | | | | |
|---|---|---|---|---|---|
| The school has a clear vision that is shared among parents, teachers, and staff | 1 | 2 | 3 | 4 | 5 |
| The school is a clean and safe environment for students and staff | 1 | 2 | 3 | 4 | 5 |
| The school involves itself in the greater community surrounding it | 1 | 2 | 3 | 4 | 5 |
| The school feels like a warm, inviting, and inclusive place | 1 | 2 | 3 | 4 | 5 |

# Schoolwide Activity Assessment

Schoolwide activities are chosen or designed for their potential to promote learning, a sense of belonging, and positive social values throughout the school community. When deciding which activities are right for your school, have your Coordinating Team consider the following questions. At the completion of an activity, ask yourselves these questions again. Were there any areas of surprise or disappointment to address?

---

## ■ *Name of Activity* ________________________________

### Does the activity promote positive social values?

Take stock of the specific values this activity will promote and those that it won't promote. Also keep in mind that activities designed to promote positive values sometimes can have unanticipated negative effects.

***Does the activity foster***

- ☐ cooperation?
- ☐ responsibility?
- ☐ interpersonal understanding?
- ☐ fairness?
- ☐ helpfulness?
- ☐ appreciation of diversity?

***Does the activity avoid***

- ☐ fostering unhealthy competitiveness?
- ☐ undermining self-esteem?
- ☐ encouraging disrespect?
- ☐ harming the environment?
- ☐ fostering materialism?

### Does the activity involve the whole school community?

While not everyone has to participate equally in every activity, over time it is important to create ways to involve all members of the school community—not just the same parents, teachers, and students that always participate.

***Does the activity have the potential to involve***

- ☐ many classrooms?
- ☐ students of different ages and abilities?
- ☐ students of all ethnic, racial, religious, and income groups?
- ☐ students whose home language is other than English?
- ☐ parents and families?
- ☐ students, parents, and staff who have not previously been involved in schoolwide activities?

# Schoolwide Activity Assessment

## Does the activity provide equal opportunity?

Some activities have built-in features that may prevent students from participating equally, but those same activities can be restructured so that all students can participate in ways that are fair and satisfying. For instance, even a very positive activity such as Adopt-a-Family could indirectly promote competition between students, if providing the "best" contribution is emphasized.

***Does the activity promote equal opportunity by***

- ☐ ensuring that all families can participate fairly (regardless of their financial status, level of English proficiency, etc.)?
- ☐ offering all students an opportunity to enhance their self-worth, rather than providing an opportunity for comparison among students?

## Does the activity give students a choice?

Students will be more likely to participate and enjoy a schoolwide activity if they have some choices about how they participate and what the goals and outcomes of the activity are. Accordingly, they will be more likely to continue to become involved in activities to the degree that they have had a sense of personal stake in the preceding ones.

***Does the activity provide students an opportunity to***

- ☐ participate in planning?
- ☐ choose roles they feel comfortable playing?
- ☐ help determine the expectations, guidelines, and outcomes of the activity?

## Does the activity contribute to a learning orientation?

Although many schoolwide activities will have a primary focus on promoting positive social values, the activities should also be consistent with, and in most cases foster, academic goals as well.

***Does the activity***

- ☐ promote a learning rather than testing orientation?
- ☐ provide opportunities for students to gain new knowledge?
- ☐ provide opportunities for parents to better understand the learning goals of the school?

## Is the activity feasible?

Some schoolwide activities may meet all the previous criteria and still simply be impossible to carry out. They may take too much teacher time or require other unavailable resources. Consider modifications or future sources of support for such activities.

***Does the activity***

- ☐ require a reasonable level of teacher energy?
- ☐ require a reasonable amount of parent participation?
- ☐ require resources the school has or can obtain?

## Are there any potential adaptations for this activity?

Activities can often be adapted to fit better with the above guidelines. Before discarding an activity that has been popular but perhaps has some shortcomings, see whether it can be altered to meet these goals.

# Questions for the Coordinating Team:
## How Are We Doing?

**Recruiting Parents:** How do we balance parent involvement on the team? How do we reach out to involve under-represented groups of parents? How do we coordinate parent volunteers?

---

**Recruiting Teachers:** How do we extend an invitation to teachers? How do we balance the team (consider grade level, role, attitudes, etc.)? How do we involve all teachers in schoolwide activities?

---

**Team Building:** How do we break down barriers and build trust and openness in order to work effectively as a group? How do we make decisions as a team?

---

**Goal Alignment:** How do we keep the group focused on the overall goal of building a more caring school community?

---

**Meetings:** When and where do we meet? How do we make sure everyone's needs are accommodated (consider time, place, language, etc.)?

---

**Communication:** How do we keep each other informed? How do we gather the input of other members of the school community (students, teachers, nonteaching staff, parents)? How do we publicize activities?

# Strategies for Increasing Parent Involvement

- Conduct an initial needs assessment through surveys, interviews, orientation and brainstorming meetings, phone calls, social gatherings, or other forums—and ask parents what they would like to see happen at the school.
- Send home several different and inviting announcements, letters, and brief reminders about each event.
- Translate print materials for families with limited English proficiency.
- Initiate a personal outreach plan. Ask parents to volunteer to call other parents and extend a personal invitation to an upcoming event, or ask each family to call another family and bring them to an upcoming event.
- Establish a parents' room or lounge that is the hub of information for parents. Encourage parent volunteers to create a welcoming environment, provide coffee, and establish a schedule of informal gatherings.
- Prepare a family newsletter that goes home with students every month.
- Involve parent volunteers in all initial planning for activities and events; ask for their input, suggestions, and assistance.
- Provide on-site translation for parents with limited English proficiency.
- Provide child care for parents with younger children.
- Provide food or snacks as part of activities for families.
- Invite individual parents to play specific roles and become actively involved in planning and organizing activities at the school.
- Make sure that you do not impose anything on parents.
- Offer information, workshops, and support for parents to help them learn more about what goes on in school and how they can reinforce what is being learned at school, both academically and socially.
- Consider the makeup of your parent population and create a wide variety of culturally appropriate opportunities for parents to become involved.
- Use teacher conferences as conversations with parents, not one-way reports.
- Offer parents many ways to experience what it's like to be in a caring community of learners.

# Additional Schoolwide Activities

The following activities are suggested ways to expand your schoolwide community-building efforts. Think about how these activities might work at your school, or add your own ideas!

---

## ☐ Goals Assembly

All students, teachers, and staff members gather together to share and affirm their goals for the year and reflect on values for the school. Students and teachers might get together in their classrooms prior to the assembly to develop their goals and an engaging way to present them to others in the assembly. A musically inclined teacher or parent might work with students to write and teach everyone a song about their goals, which can be performed to begin or end the assembly.

## ☐ Art Works

Parents volunteer and receive training in specific art techniques so they can assist in classrooms working on schoolwide art projects. These art projects can center around particular themes from literature, social studies, science, or math.

## ☐ Peer Tutoring

Upper-grade students volunteer to participate in this program and are matched with younger students to tutor. This requires very careful oversight; the student volunteers will need to understand how to be most helpful to younger students and how to avoid frustrating or upsetting them.

## ☐ Community Sing

Families learn and enjoy singing together songs from different generations and cultures. This activity is one way in which the school can recognize and learn about the cultural backgrounds of its children, families, and staff members.

## ☐ Family Arts

Families come to school in the evening to work on an art project together and learn simple activities they can do together at home.

## ☐ Community Service

Families work together on a community service project with a collaborating agency. Possibilities include a beach or park clean-up, a painting or renovation project, gardening, providing meals to homeless, maintaining a hiking trail, or visiting a nursing home.

## ☐ Person of the Week

In the classroom, randomly selecting a class member each week for special recognition helps create a feeling of togetherness and gives each child a chance to "shine." The Special Person of the Week tells others more about himself or herself, perhaps bringing in personal mementos that can be collected in a bulletin board biography. At a schoolwide level, a centrally located bulletin board could be devoted each week to featuring a class and its work. A bulletin board could also be established to feature different staff members periodically.

## ☐ End-of-Year Celebration

The entire school gathers to reflect on the year's accomplishments, celebrate good feelings, and honor the contributions of everyone in the community. Showing slides taken of everyone throughout the year is a community-building alternative to awards assemblies that promote competitive feelings and recognize only a few students.